Respondi... ....
Affections of the Lord

R. E. A. L.

JOY

Joy Chickonoski

R.E.A.L. JOY – Responding Entirely to the Affections of the Lord

©2019 Joy Chickonoski

Scripture quotations marked (NASB) are taken from the NEW AMERICAN STANDARD BIBLE', Copyright ©1960, 1962, 1963, 1968, 1971, 1972, 1973, 1975, 1977, 1995 by The Lockman Foundation. Used by permission.

Scripture quotations marked KJV are from the King James Version of the Bible (Public Domain).

Scripture quotations marked (NKJV) taken from the New King James Version®. Copyright © 1982 by Thomas Nelson, Inc. Used by permission.

Scripture quotations marked (NIV) taken from the New International Version®. Copyright © 1973, 1978, 1984, 2011 by Biblica, Inc.™ Used by permission of Zondervan. All rights reserved worldwide.

Scripture quotations marked (TLB) are taken from The Living Bible copyright © 1971 by Tyndale House Foundation. Used by permission of Tyndale House Publishers Inc.

Scripture quotations marked (ESV) are taken from The Holy Bible, English Standard Version. ESV® Text Edition: 2016. Copyright © 2001 by Crossway Bibles, a publishing ministry of Good News Publishers.

Scripture quotation marked (ASV) is taken from The American Standard Bible, Standard Domain.

Scripture quotation marked (AMP) is taken from the Amplified Bible, Copyright © 2015 by The Lockman Foundation. All rights reserved.

Scripture quotation marked (MSG) is taken from The Message, Copyright © 1993, 2002, 2018 by Eugene H. Peterson.

Some Scripture quotations are author's paraphrases.

Cover graphics designed by Perry J. Chickonoski III. To see more of his work visit Facebook.com/PJamesArtistry

Printed in the United States of America.

ISBN: 978-1-67161095-8

getrealliving.com

R.E.A.L. JOY

Responding Entirely to the Affections of the Lord

Endorsements

The world strives for happiness, which is temporary and dependent upon circumstances. God's joy is forever — no matter what we are going through in life. His joy comes from a true understanding and relationship with the One who is Joy and seeing ourselves as God created us to be in everyday life. As we accept who we are in Him, we experience His lasting joy. Joy Chickonoski leads us through a personal process of knowing God, allowing Him to change our thinking and receiving pure and everlasting joy. I encourage you to read *R.E.A.L. Joy — Responding Entirely to the Affections of the Lord* and learn how to live in the joy and rest of the Lord!

Dr. John Benefiel
Heartland Apostolic Prayer Network – Presiding Apostle
Church on the Rock, Oklahoma City – Founder and Senior Pastor

"Happy" is an adjective constantly reacting to influences either from within or outside a person. But "joy" is a noun, a state of being whose source is from God. Joy Chickonoski, in her insightful book, takes us on her real journey to finding that source of joy. This is an amazing, honest look at obstacles that steal your joy. This book is filled with God's higher wisdom and revelation, often challenging you. I highly recommend this as a foundational tool to all desiring to get R.E.A.L. with God!

Dr. Yolanda McCune
HAPN Kingdom Culture Director

As I began to read **R.E.A.L. Joy**, I could see that this is a book of healing — mind, body, and spirit. As a counselor, I believe those who really step into this book will be able to do what I say, "Step out, step up, step over, to one's destiny", because, without one's joy, one cannot receive. I certainly recommend to all those who feel lost to read and pay close attention to **R.E.A.L. Joy**.

Dr. Negiel Bigpond
HAPN First Nations Director

R.E.A.L. Joy will guide you along the most important journey of your life into knowing the Father's delight for your created purpose. Joy teaches from life experience as a prophet and visionary, as well as from other leaders' inspiring teachings that propelled her vision. Matthew 5:8, "Blessed are the pure in heart for they will see God," will be the blessing in your life as you learn these crucial life lessons.

Abby Abildness
Global Apostolic Prayer Network Leader
Executive Director of Healing Tree International

Father has fashioned and designed each vessel He has created to contain and manifest His glory in special and unique ways.

He then names that container, so the fullness of that name, when submitted to the prompts of the Master's gentle touch, unfolds in perfect time different measures of the fragrance, intensity of colors of glory, and sweet refrain of melodies of Heaven the container was created to release from the foundation.

In John 10:10, Lord Jesus tells us that the enemy does everything within his power to steal, kill, and destroy every intended purpose of that vessel.

Joy Chickonoski is a vessel that has discovered who she is and releases with great intensity and boldness the glory Elohiym has placed within her! In order to manifest what she was created from the foundation to release, she has had to confront many moments when the enemy of her destiny was screaming that she was everything but JOY! But the Father, who created her, made no mistake when He fashioned and named her after His strength!

So yes, this Joy Chickonoski is a glorious container of the joy of His strength, but not just any container, the kingdom substance she releases is bright, bold, delivering joy! So let the blood-bought Victory she has been fashioned to carry, help fashion the strength of Father's JOY in You.

James Nesbit

When Joy's book found me, I had a broken heart and I was weary. By faith, I took a joyride with Father, Son and Holy Spirit. I found a Kingdom AAA TripTik. So I was on a journey with stops to feast at banquets of the fruit of the Spirit. At the end of my joyride, every cell in my body was infused with rich and deep, eternal joy.

Therese Thurston, HAPN Apostolic Leader for Ohio.
Co-Host Science and Wonders Podcast

It is with great pleasure that I endorse Joy's latest book, **R.E.A.L. Joy**; an authentic, practical approach to harnessing the power of the joy of the Lord in your life. The personal and interactive experiences will relate to you. This book is a message that Joy Chickonoski embodies and imparts to her reader.

Faisal Malick
Lead Pastor, www.covenantoflife.org
Founder and President, www.plumblinenetwork.com

In the book *R.E.A.L. Joy*, Joy takes you on a journey of intimacy and surrender to find the ultimate joy in life. Reading about her journey will challenge you in your own journey with God so you can find your way into the deep with all He has planned for you. It will encourage you to listen to the voice of God, dream with God, and find new adventures into your destiny with real joy.

Pastor Kathie Thomas
Victory Christian Center

In Joy Chickonoski's latest book, *R.E.A.L. Joy*, she doesn't just talk about what joy is, she gives you real-life experiences. She takes you along on her personal journey through the scriptures, demonstrating how God has helped her to discover *R.E.A.L. Joy* in the process. It's not all about theology, but rather Joy helps you connect with God personally, allowing Him to produce *R.E.A.L. Joy* in you.

Bishop Robert Stearns
Executive Director of Eagles' Wings, NY

Dedication

Being a female prophet in my own hometown has been a challenge, to say the least. Many times, I have attempted to argue with the Lord, stating that even He could not be a prophet in His own hometown, and I am a woman too! He would smile and say, "This is a 'greater works will you do' opportunity!"

In the darkest, loneliest moments of grief and disappointment, my husband Perry has been Jesus in the flesh to me. But many times, we both needed to know we weren't crazy and God was speaking to us.

Teri and Paul Moser have been our safe place.

It is my delight to dedicate this book to them.

Teri is my sister, and both she and Paul have been our governing leaders and partners in ministry. But more importantly, they have been in deep covenant relationship with us in life and friendship. They are the ones Perry and I rely on to hear our hearts, hear from God, and help us process the revelation and pain in being forerunners for the Apostolic reformation. They have brought **R.E.A.L. Joy** into my life. I am so grateful.

Acknowledgments

Of course, I want to start by thanking Father for speaking to me and giving me the privilege and responsibility of communicating His heart to His children. *I am honored to partner with Jesus* in the adventure of Kingdom work. *Thank you to Holy Spirit,* who has guided and directed me in life and in writing this book.

I have so many people to thank, as well; first and foremost, I thank my husband Perry and children Carley, Cami and Perry. They have witnessed firsthand the grace and mercy of God at work in my life through all "the stuff."

I want to thank my Administrator, Star Wileman. She sure does make me look good, and without her, I would be years behind in accomplishing the call of God on my life.

Thank you to Michelle Napolitano, David Moser and Carol Martinez for all their hard work in bringing this project to light.

I am blessed to be the daughter of Pastor Jim and Georgia Leone, the godly heritage I get to walk in is because of their faithful walk with the Lord. Thank you for being a part of our journey and ministry.

To my siblings, Jim and Betty, Nicole and Anthony, Teri and Paul, who are a part of our ministry and calling, thank you for sticking it out. I know it has been tough at times, but we have learned how to walk in the five-fold ministry together, and I am so looking forward to what the Lord is going to do in us and for us… together.

Perry and I love doing life and ministry with all our family, kids, nieces and nephews, and cousins… It's a great family "business" to be doing the business of the Kingdom together.

Thank you so much to our RLM Family; we are honored to lead and serve the amazing people of Real Living Ministries.

Table of Contents

Foreword

Come along on an adventure with me... we will access Kingdom power together as we walk by faith and not by sight. This book is filled with adventures. It's a joy ride with God. In a world that demands understanding while giving none, Christianity must be more than a good argument. It must be a real experience with genuine love and practical answers that are filled with wonder.

Several years ago, while teaching a class called "Fearless Parenting in a Scary World," I assembled a panel of young adults for a question and answer time. This panel consisted of Christian youth, some raised by Christians and some not.

One woman asked my son, who was 20 at the time and on the panel, if his Christian friends he grew up with were still walking with God, and if not, what made the difference in his life. His response was interesting. He said, "Not many of my friends who grew up in Christian homes ever really walked with God themselves. I will tell you, in my opinion, why not." He said, "My parents made being a Christian fun. My friends went to church because they had to, but I wanted to. It was an adventure and still is."

So let's have some fun! I have to be honest and tell you that my intention was to ask someone who is well-known to do the foreword for this book. I thought that person would open doors that I am not capable of opening. Well, I asked, but as you can see, that didn't work out. I now know why... let me show you.

Come with me to my back deck in the middle of the woods in Youngstown, Ohio. It was a sunny, warm morning, which is a treat where I live. I was basking in the sun, while immersed in the delight of the Lord as I worshipped and enjoyed His presence. All of a sudden, I saw myself in the spirit sitting at a beautiful table. I was feeling both gratitude and intimidation. Jesus approached me and invited me to sit next to Him at the head of the table. I shook my head and motioned to Him that I was fine where I was. He insisted, and I quoted scripture to him… really. I tried to say that I was not going to take the seat of honor; that I was following the Bible and would take the seat of dishonor. He bent in close to me and said rather sternly, "You were told to do that until asked to take the seat of honor; now get up!"

It was a chilling rebuke but not enough to move me, believe it or not. I sat there frozen and cried for several minutes. I repented for not being able to move. Jesus said, "You do not even see the table you are at. You are no longer among critics and this seat I offer you is not fought over at this table." I realized the people I was with were happy to see me being invited to sit next to Jesus and they wanted to celebrate what Jesus was doing in my life. I had the sense that these people had taken their turn and knew they would return to the seat of honor again at the Lord's request. Knowing this, they were not competing for the seat of honor and were not critical of the person seated. Being humbled by the experience, I rose to take the seat. Once seated, I realized I had a unique table setting with my own food and centerpiece tailored to my style and tastes as well as did the others. We were all seated next to Him. It appeared we were all seated at the same table and yet at our own tables at the same time. No one was in need of impressing God or the others at the table. We were uniquely one. Unity brings joy, but it must be oneness, not sameness.

It must be a celebration and not a competition. Sonship empowers me to do justly among men, love mercy and walk humbly with God (Micah 6:8).

So, here I am, seated at my unique table of the Lord. I invite you to come up alongside me with your unique table, and let's celebrate Jesus together. You will read later in this book about the table I used to be at and the pain and joy I have walked in along my journey with God.

This experience on my back deck, just weeks before I published this book, is why I knew I had to write my own foreword. I needed to let go of the fear of personal opinions and not hide behind someone I deem more honorable. I needed to come to the table knowing Jesus has invited me to share my story.

R. E. A. L.

JOY

Let's Get Acquainted

Chapter I

Discovering Joy...
Joy Chickonoski

Some of my fondest childhood memories are of bike-riding in Mill Creek Park. My mom would pack our lunches, then my brother and I would head out for a full day of adventures. The park was filled with winding roads, shaded picnic tables and babbling brooks with plenty of hiding places to meet up with friends. We would catch crawfish, skip stones and race each other home, full of laughter. However, when I was ten, we moved too far from the park to go on my own… I found other friends and other interests. But at sixteen, armed with a newly minted driver's license and keys in hand, the park was my go-to place again.

I was here once again with a specific plan: This time, I would meet up with God. I had been coming to this spot in the park for my devotions ever since I had obtained my driver's license, but this day was different. As I sat at the foot of the waterfall, Father asked me why I loved to come here. I closed my eyes, looking up to feel the warmth of the sun, and smiled. Then I replied, "I love the sound of the waterfall; it blocks out the chaos so I can hear you." Father spoke softly, "Would you like to hear and feel that sound of peace anytime you wish?" "Of course," was my reply.

Then, it happened. I felt the waterfall move into my spirit, and the sound of it began echoing on the inside. My spirit began to sing Psalm 93:4, "Mightier than the thunder of the waters the Lord my God is mighty."

I knew things would be different. I had found access to the secret place (Psalm 91), and from now on, I could run into God for refuge anytime and anywhere. After that, I no longer had the need to go to the waterfall in the park. It wasn't long after, that the path to the bottom of the falls closed due to erosion. God is so good!

Looking back at that time in my life, I realize the intentionality of Trinity; each One moving me towards greater intimacy. Father knew I needed healing regarding the way I thought of His love and expectations for my life. Jesus knew I valued suffering more than resurrection, and that caused me to view life painfully rather than joyfully. Holy Spirit knew I had gifts that framed the way I viewed others and only intimacy with Him would expand that.

Hindsight is 20/20, right? But for decades, I went through valleys and climbed mountains and hung on cliffs, waiting to be rescued. Often I felt abandoned, orphaned, and angry at God. Now, I look back and can see Trinity was bringing me back to the Garden of Eden, back to his original intentions for humanity, back to my destiny. Psalms 139: 13-16 states:

> For you formed my inward parts;
> you knitted me together in my mother's womb.
> I praise you, for I am fearfully and wonderfully made.
> Wonderful are your works; my soul knows it very well.
> My frame was not hidden from you,
> when I was being made in secret,

intricately woven in the depths of the earth.
Your eyes saw my unformed substance;
in your book were written, every one of them,
the days that were formed for me,
when as yet there was none of them. (*ESV*)

David knew God had a specific intention for his life and fashioned him in his mother's womb with that destiny in mind. He also had a sense that his spirit knew his destiny and agreed to it before he was born.

God tells Jeremiah the same thing in Jeremiah 1:5-10:

"Before I formed you in the womb I knew you,
and before you were born I consecrated you;
I appointed you a prophet to the nations."
Then I said, "Ah, Lord God! Behold, I do not know how
to speak, for I am only a youth." But the Lord said to me,
"Do not say, 'I am only a youth'; for to all to whom I send you,
you shall go, and whatever I command you, you shall speak.
Do not be afraid of them, for I am with you to deliver you,
declares the Lord." Then the Lord put out his hand
and touched my mouth. And the Lord said to me,
"Behold, I have put my words in your mouth.
See, I have set you this day over nations and over kingdoms." (*ESV*)

In this passage, God reminds Jeremiah that he agreed to his destiny before he was formed in his mother's womb. God did not allow Jeremiah to discredit his calling because of his insecurity. Instead, God, speaking prophetically, took Jeremiah back to his future. He reminded him of what happened in the Garden before he came to earth, and then showed him how he would walk that out in the earth!

We are all on a journey "back to the future." Even before we were born, our spirit said "yes" to God's plan. We are learning to walk according to the Spirit and not the flesh.

We are all on a journey back to the future. Our spirit said "yes" to God's plan.

Nearly four decades have passed since that day I started my journey to R.E.A.L. Joy. That day at the waterfall, I entered the secret place of the Most High God (Psalm 91) and began the journey of discovering who Joy Leone (later to become Joy Chickonoski) really is. In all that I have experienced, I have come to say, as "the Beloved" of Song of Solomon (4:16):

> Awake, O north wind, And come, O south!
> Blow upon my garden, That its spices may flow out.
> Let my beloved come to his garden And eat its pleasant fruits. (NKJV)

The journey back to who we were meant to be is filled with ups and downs, blessings and trials. These are represented poetically in this scripture from the Song of Solomon as the cold winds of the north and the warm winds of the south. Intimacy with Trinity, expressed uniquely in each person of the Godhead, must be our focus. The Beloved in Song of Solomon had learned the importance of letting both the trial and blessing release the spices of her worship and love for God, attracting Him to draw nearer to her. She longed to discover more of who God is rather than focus on her situation. The Beloved learned her ability to hold on to God's affections, which is what attracted Him to her, allowing her to become more intimate with Him in every situation.

During worship one evening, Father showed me a bright fuchsia pink torch that was lighting up the darkness. He said, "This is the color of the joy of the Lord. It will strengthen you and light your way."

He then showed me the formula and importance of the color I was seeing. First, I noticed the color had a metallic effect, which is the base of the color for joy. The Lord said this effect, which can create a steel shimmer, represents the pain in life from which joy grows. Then He showed me scarlet red, which represents the blood of Jesus and His grace in our pain. Then He added white to the color to make it fuchsia pink. He said, "When my children rely on my grace in their pain, their hearts are purified from the things that steal true joy." The joy of the Lord comes from leaning into God during painful times, **Responding Entirely to the Affections of the Lord (R.E.A.L.)** and receiving His perspective!

Along our journey together, as you read, I will leave you torch reminders, leading you to the joy of the Lord.

In your mind's eye, see splashes of bright fuchsia on the words and meditate on them to receive the joy of the Lord.

I have realized my name is Joy because I am called to bring people into the joy of intimacy with Trinity. Like the Shulamite woman of Song of Solomon, I have discovered the joy of contentment in the will of God. I am no longer consumed with figuring out the 'why' of my circumstances, but only the 'who'. I no longer need to know why God does or does not do certain things. Instead, I find great joy in discovering who God desires to be for me or who He sees me to be in each situation. My journey in discovering who Trinity is, and who they say Joy Chickonoski is, has led me to discover *R.E.A.L. JOY.*

Chapter 2

Time to Get Real (The Backstory)

As soon as I woke up one sunny day in May 2007, the Lord said, "We are going for a little ride."

"Ok," I replied. I immediately got dressed and jumped in the car. I love adventures with Jesus! I drove until I reached an abandoned strip plaza. Then Jesus said, "Turn in here." So, I parked in front and Jesus asked, "What would you do with this building if I gave it to you?" WOW! I started dreaming with Jesus about all the cool ministries we could start. My heart was racing. Then it came. "You are going to resign your position as associate pastor and start your own ministry."

Wait... What? No... it can't be! My mind began to race. I had been the associate pastor of High Pointe for fifteen years, alongside dear friends who had been the senior pastors. We were in covenant, with a history dating back to grade school. We had been through so much together; there was no way we could leave them now. I dreamed of my daughters walking down the aisle in the church's new worship center we had just finished building. *I can't be leaving now,* I protested within. I sat there in that parking lot, stunned, with tears and panic overwhelming me. In that moment, I felt as alone as the abandoned plaza I was staring at.

My husband was at work; I could not possibly drop this bomb on him in the middle of his day. All my family and closest friends went to my church, so I couldn't involve them before my Pastor knew. Oh! But my sister Teri, our worship leader, and her new husband, Paul, were on a three-month sabbatical. Since technically they were not going to our church, I gave them a call. I was expecting them to talk some sense into me; they loved our church as much as I did. After I shared, Teri told me, "Paul just woke me up this morning and said, 'Get Joy on the phone; she is starting her own ministry, and we are going with her.'" What!

Here we go… a God moment when we realize He has been hard at work behind the scenes in our life. God truly is a Maestro orchestrating the seemingly random pieces of our lives into one beautiful sound. We need to be open to the fullness of God's sovereignty as "He changes the times and seasons…" (Daniel 2:21 *NIV*). We often tell God He can do whatever He wants with our lives, but in reality, we have handed Him a coloring book crafted by our own ideas. We expect Him to color inside the lines.

Stop here for a moment and think about your life. What is God doing behind the scenes? He is trying to create something beautiful. Maybe it is hard to see because He is coloring outside of the lines you penned for Him. Journal with Holy Spirit and let Him show you what He is thinking.

That day in the parking lot, God handed me back my coloring book and showed me His own ideas. Teri, Paul and I decided to meet for lunch in a secluded, newer restaurant out of the area, where no one would recognize us. We had a lot to talk about! As we walked in the door, there sat my parents. Unbelievable! In this moment, I could see God's hand. The Maestro was still at work. Relief and divine assurance came over me.

My father is a five-fold (see Ephesians 4:11) teacher/pastor, and I am a five-fold prophet. Seeing eye-to-eye does not come easy for us, to say the least. For the first time, I was actually excited for what I thought was about to happen. Most of the time, when I hear from God and go flying off, my dad tries to ground me. Often after this agonizing process, we both jokingly laugh about how God transforms us. This time was different. I was longing for my dad's practical gifting as teacher/pastor to ground me. I wanted my dad to pull me out of this cloud and talk some sense into me. I told them everything. Surprisingly, Dad said, "Yes, and you're going to do it at the YMCA!" This was not what I wanted to hear. Certainly it made sense to go there. I had been teaching a women's Bible study and serving as the Christian Emphasis Coordinator at our local YMCA for several years. I had a great relationship with the staff who fully embraced and supported everything we were doing there.

Wow! Is this really going to happen? As I started to think about the process Perry and I had been in for several years, it all started to come together.

The Lord had already positioned us for a transition several years before. Father asked us to resign our positions at our church to step down from paid staff and serve as volunteers. We were serving in this capacity with much less responsibility. At the time, we felt we were doing this as a contribution to the building fund and to prioritize the growing needs of our family.

Then, several weeks prior to the shocking notice regarding leaving the church, Perry and I were in our yard getting it ready for spring. We both looked up at each other at the same time and said, "It's time to make our own mistakes." We knew the calling to serve as associates and volunteers was lifting, but we thought our senior pastor was leaving, and the Lord was preparing us to take the lead of High

Pointe. So, we had scheduled an appointment to speak frankly with our pastor.

Later that evening, Perry and I sat down and I shared with him all that happened on my adventure with Jesus and lunch with my family. Then the phone rang. It was my sister-in-law, who had been trying to reach me for days. Betty began by saying, "I saw Dad tonight and he acted strangely when I told him about the dream I had. The one I have been trying to tell you about. What is going on, Joy?"

"I am not at liberty to say, but what was your dream?" I replied.

Betty dreamt that we were having meetings at the YMCA and people were coming from all over to get saved, delivered and healed. "We have to start a church at the Y," she told me urgently.

"Betty, the Lord told me today I was leaving our church to start a ministry at the Y!" I said tearfully, "But you can't come. I am not going to take good leadership from out of our church. Perry and I are leaving alone. We have no idea what this is all about!"

She said, "You can't do that to me!"

At this point I was scared. I didn't want to hurt my church or my pastor in any way! I cried out, "Father, what are you doing!"

The day of our scheduled meeting with our pastor arrived. We needed to tell him that we were leaving. Never in a million years had I thought this would happen. We had pledged to be with them even if everyone else left! Pastor Tony had an evangelist heart and focused on the nearly saved and barely saved. I was a prophet who stirred up the waters of revival and all the gifts of the Spirit. We rode the waves of these two very different approaches to church life pretty well together. However, neither of us was really seeing what we wanted. We kept deferring to each other. We had learned a lot about five-fold ministry and grown as Christians together. Now it was time for us to have our ministry dreams come true. It was hard to realize we were holding each other back.

After sharing with Pastor Tony, Perry told him, "We are leaving alone. We do not want anyone coming with us. We have no idea what this even is. God told us to just stop doing everything we know how to do. We are not starting a church. We don't know what we are doing. It's an Abrahamic journey; we just need to leave without knowing where we are going."

It's an Abrahamic journey; we just need to leave without knowing where we are going.

Pastor Tony said, "I appreciate your heart and I know your heart for this church and our covenant relationship. But I can't let you do that. I know there are people God is calling to come with you. I won't hold them back."

I still cry all these years later. Covenant is so powerful. Trusting and honoring each other through good and bad is what the kingdom of God is all about. Pastor Tony, sometime later, also answered God's call to move to a different state, and is currently the lead Associate Pastor of a very evangelistic church of over 4,000 people. He too is living his dream!

Perry, Pastor Tony and I agreed to pray and ask God for a list of people we felt were to come with us. We each made our own list, without consulting one another, and agreed that we would only ask those who were on all three of our lists. We each had the same exact list.

Several weeks later, High Pointe released a team of eleven missionaries and their children to our local YMCA.

At the time, here is all the blueprint we had...

- **First, we were to stop doing everything we knew how to do concerning church life and church leadership.** The team we assembled were all seasoned leaders and worshippers. As you can imagine, there was a lot we had to stop doing.

- **Second, we were to focus on prayer, fasting, worship and the Word.** Anything beyond that was off limits. We had to rediscover the purity and beauty of intimacy with Father without any of the enhancements and sophistications of modern church life.

- **Next, we were not allowed to advertise or invite anyone else to join until further notice.** God was calling us to something so foreign to anything we'd ever been a part of, and He knew that adding more people would become a distraction to us from this calling.

- **Last, we were to use the tithe for equipping the saints rather than getting people saved.** So, we created a storehouse fund to equip us for our future, whatever that would be. We sent our team to various conferences and bought curriculum as we were led. God wanted us to learn. He wanted to spend His money on us! That was so foreign. Our collective ministry experience taught us that the leadership gets used and abused for the sake of the unfaithful, unsaved, nearly saved, barely saved. All the while, the leadership gets burnt out. We were convinced this is what God expected of church leadership. Looking back, we had a lot to learn about God's heart towards us.

Now, we "2 Timothy 2:2" it to the World.

The things which you have heard from me in the presence of many witnesses, entrust these to faithful men who will be able to teach others also. (*NASB*)

The tithe would be spent to equip the saints for the work of ministry. Outreach to lost souls would then be done on a personal one-on-one basis by those trained to be kingdom-minded in the marketplace.

We were not building a church; we were building a team — a team that would eventually build the city. We were not building a location for a church but building what the New Testament calls the *ecclesia*, which translates as church. Apostle Paul understood the ecclesia to be a group of Christ-followers equipped to minister out of the gifts and offices of the Spirit for the purpose of establishing Heaven's Kingdom on earth.

When the time came to invite others into our fellowship, we were not to focus on how to keep them. God did not want prisons. We were training people for Kingdom work. It was between them and God how long they stayed.

A major shift took place in our perspective regarding Sunday morning service. This special time together was not meant for the people. It was meant for God. He was the guest that we were to focus on keeping! We needed to create a safe place for Holy Spirit to come and be who He was without worrying how people were going to feel about it. Today, our passion for people is secondary to our passion for God's presence.

We were to listen to God, then do what He said regardless of the cost.

God then took me to 2 Kings 19:29, and I knew our ministry would have three seasons to its inception:

> And this shall be a sign unto thee, Ye shall eat this year such things as grow of themselves, and in the second year that which springeth of the same; and in the third year sow ye, and reap, and plant vineyards, and eat the fruits thereof. (KJV)

"Eat this year such things as grow of themselves." We spent the first three years eating what grew on its own. This meant we invested in our own personal growth and revival. We knew God had something very different for us. We needed our minds renewed by Holy Spirit. We needed new visions of God's heart for us. We needed to protect what God was doing in us. So, carefully and sometimes painfully, we did not invite anyone to join us during this season. At the time, we called ourselves the renegade group because the word "renegade" means a deserter of status quo. It was difficult to explain to others what we were doing, so a lot of misunderstanding was out there. But we just kept obeying God.

During this first season, He gave us our mission statement and ministry title — Real Living Ministries (RLM). R.E.A.L. is an acronym for **Responding Entirely to the Affections of the Lord**. Our mission was to get R.E.A.L. with God, ourselves and others. God began to reveal to us that we were suffering from what I called at the time an Illegitimate Spirit; something that is now commonly referred to as the Orphan Spirit. We were learning how to respond to God's affections instead of listening to lies of the enemy concerning who God was and how He felt about who we were.

"In the second year that which springeth of the same..." We spent the next season of four years eating that which started springing

up in our hearts. As a result of all the healing and personal growth of the previous three years, new fruit began springing forth. Perry, a five-fold Apostle, discerned that this new season was upon us, and it was time to involve others in what we were doing.

In January 2010, we launched the Decade of the Seer. According to Jeremiah 1:11-13 and 1 Samuel 9:9, a seer is a prophet or person who hears from God in picture form in their mind's eye or imagination. This happens through dreams and visions. It is interesting to note that God does not ask Jeremiah what he feels or thinks but what he actually sees. Seers also see patterns in nature that reveal God's heart towards humanity. Jesus was acting as a seer when He spoke in parables. He used well-known shared experiences of the culture to say, "The Kingdom of Heaven is like…"

In 2010, God began to increase our abilities to walk with the Holy Spirit in the supernatural realms. It was during this season that we learned about quantum physics and how God was allowing man to see how He does things in the invisible realms.

In addition, over the years, I had received a number of prophetic words that I would have a counseling center. Back in the late 80s I had learned about Theophostic Ministry, which is a prayerful technique for inner-healing which allows Jesus to show up and shine His light on old memories and wounds. This is how God had been speaking to me personally for years. Theophostic Ministry inspired me to teach others how to connect with God the way I had been for quite some time. I have also been a seer since I was very young. From an early age, Jesus would come to me through my imagination or through nature, as He did at the waterfall. Over the years, I developed "Unreeling," a unique way of doing inner healing by using the imagination.

Romans 12:2 tells us to be transformed by the renewing of our minds. Holy Spirit has shown me how to create an environment where people feel safe to invite Jesus into their painful memories. He edits the movie reel of the mind, giving them a new way to see and remember.

Thus, in 2010, we started what God told me to call the RLM Life Coaching Center. At the time, I did not know that a Life Coach would soon become a recognized profession. It wasn't a title I knew at the time; it was only the name He gave me for our pastoral counseling center. Our mode has always been to simply listen to God and do what He says, no matter the cost. You don't have to know all the details because He does. It's so much easier when you surrender and just obey.

In 2015 we stepped into the third season of sowing and reaping. We became Apostolic leaders of Heartland Apostolic Prayer Network (HAPN). Suddenly, we learned what God had been calling us to do all along. All these years, we had been stepping into totally different ways to do church, simply by listening and obeying. It was only after we had developed our ministry that we learned we were an Apostolic Center. We were sitting in our first annual leaders' gathering for HAPN. They began to share about the differences between a church and an Apostolic Center. It was unbelievable to see that was what God had been changing our ministry into! We had made every single change, and no one but Holy Spirit had taught us these things.

God has always been faithful to confirm that we've been on the right track through connecting us with others who are doing the same things. I am so grateful to men like Bill Johnson, Kris Vallotton and Danny Silk who gave us the confidence we needed to pursue the new ideas we had through their books on honor and the supernatural. I am so grateful for Patricia King, who assured me that God was using women to be prophets to the nation! For years, I obeyed and was greatly criticized, even condemned for my stance. Mike Bickle, thank you for showing me it was ok to focus on the superior pleasures of relationship with Jesus instead of merely trying to convince people to stop pursuing the inferior pleasures of sin. I will never forget the day I read in one of Rick Joyner's books that God was raising up a company of Elijahs on the earth! I thought I was hearing from God when He kept telling me I was like Elijah, but I questioned it all the time. I finally accepted it that day. I learned a great deal about how to be a godly prophet from Rick Joyner and so many others.

So it was very fitting and unexpected that the week before we started our new Ministry in 2007, I got to be a part of a graduation ceremony at Morning Star Ministries (Rick Joyner's church). My family and I had planned our summer vacation for the first week in June, long before we knew we would leave the Monday after our last Sunday at High Pointe. On our way home after our vacation week, we decided to go to Rick Joyner's Sunday morning service. It just so happened to be their graduation ceremony for their school of ministry. Holy Spirit spoke and said to me, "You have graduated training and are now one of my prophets!" You just can't make that kind of stuff up! I love walking with God!

> *Eagles, the mature saints who are ahead of us, are*
> *there to encourage our faith — not create it!*

They are there to help you articulate what is already in your heart or ignite a passion for more of God. Never try to do something simply because it worked out well for someone else. The Holy Spirit wants you to walk by faith with His personal guidance. Your calling is unique. You are fearfully and wonderfully made. You will fall short of who you really are if you pursue the callings and revelation in someone else's life. God has something just for you. Let the eagles inspire you, not control you.

I have a good memory and can remember quite well teachings and quotes from books that have impacted me. But journaling is one of the greatest ways to grow spiritually. Especially if you do not have a good memory. Read your books devotionally, highlighting that which really speaks to you and making notes in your journal regarding these. This is how to let others impact your life and not just make an impression with their wisdom. Also, hold on to those books that have most impacted you. I remember being led to reread Francis Frangipane's book, *Battlefield of the Mind,* that I had first read in the late 80s. I wept as I realized all the change that had happened in my life and heart that had stemmed from reading that book!

Journal. Keep it. Holy Spirit will take you back to it.

I am also so grateful for Francis, who took a chance on me and published my first book. I didn't realize at the time that *Becoming Lovers: The Journey from Disciple of Christ to Bride of Christ* would outline the twelve cultures of Real Living Ministries and become the foundation for all we teach in our ministry. I released that book in January 2007, just months before we were sent on our Abrahamic journey.

The American culture is so fast-paced; we want everything yesterday. According to scripture, patience in the little things is what makes you master over much. But Americans have little time for the little things! Yet again, scripture teaches that God uses the foolish things to confound the wise. I am so grateful that God kept me faithful to slowly grow our ministry with purpose. Again, while everyone was reading books that stated if a ministry doesn't grow in numbers in three years, it never will (a stupid American idea for sure), God was telling us not to focus on "getting" people. Everything He was leading us to do defied common knowledge, and I definitely felt foolish! But, in 2013, while at a Pastors Conference at Bethel in Redding, California, Perry and I received a powerful prophetic word. We were told, "While many are growing gardens that spring up quickly but have constant turnover and require great effort to maintain, you are growing an orchard." They continued to say, "An orchard, once planted, takes 7-10 years to produce fruit. But once it starts growing fruit, it does not stop and requires very little effort to maintain."

WOW! Our hearts soared, not because we wanted to make that happen, but rather we knew it *was* happening. We just didn't understand why until God gave us that word.

Defining Greatness

I have always known that God wanted to do great things with my life. The same is true for all of our lives. But over the years, Holy Spirit had helped me to rearrange the way I defined greatness. When my children were little, I had an encounter with Father that set a plumb line in my life for many years. I was reading a book about Kathryn Kuhlman, someone I have valued since I was a little girl. I remember watching her on TV with my grandmother. My hometown was one of three places in which Kathryn ministered regularly. I was supernaturally healed as an infant from spinal meningitis under the healing anointing in our town from her ministry.

As I read her book, I went into an activation or vision: I was sitting in a Kathryn Kuhlman service at Stambaugh Auditorium in Youngstown, Ohio. I could see her vividly pacing back and forth on the stage. Then she invited all the pastors in the congregation to join her on the stage. We all filed out of our seats and formed a semi-circle behind her on the stage. I was one of about 30 that came up. I could see her preaching with her back to us as we faced the audience. Then she spun around and started pointing her finger at all of us pastors behind her. She said repeatedly, "Somebody wants my anointing. Who is it?" Finally, she came right up to me with her finger in my face and said, "It's you, isn't it?" I nodded yes, fearfully. She said, "Are you willing to pay the price?" I said, "No ma'am." To my surprise she said, "Good. Now stick out your hands." I did. Fire went through my body when she touched me, and I wept for nearly an hour.

You may be reading this thinking, *Wait; there must be a typo. This says Joy said, "No, ma'am!"* It's not a typo! Kathryn paid a price, along with many other revivalists, that I was unwilling and still am unwilling to pay. At the height of her ministry, she was divorced and the spiritual warfare that surrounded her life so exhausted her that at the end she didn't want prayer for healing in her own life because she was so tired! I know many look at that as a brave sacrifice. I see it as a bad trade with the devil! I am not trying to be critical here, but I think we can learn from mistakes as well as success in life.

I have a passion for the family and see that many in full-time ministry sacrifice their own children and marriages on the altar of ministry. Paul states in 1 Corinthians chapter 7:32,33 that it is better to remain single so you can mind the things of the Lord. For if you marry, you must mind the things of the world, such as how to please your spouse. Paul knew having a family would affect what you could do for the Lord.

I do not believe that supernatural anointing needs to cost us our families and health, but it often does. Unfortunately, pastors' kids are notorious for being the most rebellious in the church. God, of course, has not designed it that way; the enemy has! I will talk a lot more on this in another chapter. For now, you need to know that I

Real Joy comes, not because we have pursued it, but rather because we have pursued God and His affections in the midst of difficulty.

made the commitment to raise my children first in the ministry and I asked God not to give me outside influence until my kids were secure in their own walk with God.

I can tell you that many times I was overwhelmed with discouragement when it appeared as if God had forgotten me. What was I doing wrong that nothing significant was happening in our ministry from my perspective? Father God would remind me, "Didn't you tell me not to give you influence until the right time?" Remember, we each have a unique calling given to us before birth according to Jeremiah. The devil is crafty and will attempt as He did with Jesus (Matthew 4) to get us to compromise our calling. Today, as I pen this manuscript, I have three adult children who are all on fire for God doing His work. At the time of this writing, my 21-year-old son Perry is training to be our worship leader. My 24-year-old daughter Carley is on our global staff and leading a young adult revival in our ministry. My 23-year-old daughter Cami is presently raising funds for her year-long mission trip to the 10/40 window nations. I am grateful every day that God has remained faithful to my request (even when the devil was enticing me to choose his way). Now I, along with one of my staff members, hold a position with HAPN as their National Leader for the Family Mountain.

As a prophet, authenticity is high priority; therefore, I want you to know the things I share in this book comes from R.E.A.L. Living. I am going to tell you about the blessings and the hardships in my life to inspire you to seek out R.E.A.L. Living for yourself. In this book, you will learn or have it confirmed to you that R.E.A.L. Joy is often birthed in pain, not just blessing. I will reveal the secrets to R.E.A.L. Joy and help define the purpose for your own battles. It is my passion to share my story as a portal into your own life. May you see Father, Jesus and Holy Spirit more clearly at work in your life as I share mine.

Let's go on a JOY RIDE with God together!

Chapter 3

Responding Entirely to the Affections of the Lord

I know that I am called to release R.E.A.L. Joy. This is the kind of deep, lasting joy that emerges from being able to Respond Entirely to the Affections of the Lord. R.E.A.L. Joy is very different from the pursuit of happiness. R.E.A.L. Joy comes, not because we have sought it, but rather because we have sought God's affections in the midst of difficulty instead of seeking happiness. Joy is not a pleasant emotion brought on by desired circumstances: that is happiness, and it is fleeting, as we all know. R.E.A.L. Joy is contentment in the will of God. It comes despite pain. Happiness is destroyed by pain. Joy does not fear pain but uses it for the good. Happiness sees no good in pain and finds discomfort in those who do.

This book is a journey in discovering R.E.A.L. Joy amidst the distraction of pleasure and pain. I have learned that pleasure is inferior to real joy, and only those who pursue happiness instead of the will of God will settle for it. I have learned to embrace pain as my cross, leading to fellowship with Christ, the ultimate joy! We will talk at length throughout this book on these subtle but important differences between happiness and R.E.A.L. Joy.

If you are a born-again believer in Jesus Christ, you already have R.E.A.L. Joy. It cannot be pursued because you already have it, but it can be stolen by the enemy when we exchange it for the pursuit of happiness. Learning to get R.E.A.L. is painful, but the reward of lasting joy is worth it. As you continue to read, I will share some of the amazing truths and experiences familiar to those who choose to pursue God rather than happiness. We will talk about God's affections, how He reveals them to us, how to respond to them and what it takes to find R.E.A.L. Joy even if your world is unhappy at the moment.

Keep It REAL in Order to Experience R.E.A.L. Joy

Being a prophet, I am all about keeping it real. I can't stand the elephant in the room; that which no one wants to talk about. You may have made friends with that elephant, preferring not to deal with conflict. If so, as you read, ask Holy Spirit to help you accept what He needs you to accept, even if what I am saying is hard to hear. Scripture warns us to be aware, lest we entertain angels unaware (Hebrews 13:2). I believe that "elephant" can be a demonic angel we are entertaining. He is sure getting a laugh out of us at times!

So, why do we have so much trouble being authentic? Why do we hide our feelings? Well, I am sure right now your mind is racing with lots of reasons. Memories of those who hurt you or misunderstood you or even abused and condemned you. Those memories remind you not to trust so easily. Some of you may be thinking, "Oh, I am fine! I keep it real." For you, I hope that is true. But it has been my experience as a pastor, prophet, apostolic leader and life coach that most people who think they are fine and have no trouble with authentic living are the most in need of healing. **Our minds try to protect us by shutting down our self-awareness.** We are hurt, insecure, and often afraid, without being aware. We are entertaining deception and it is stealing R.E.A.L. Joy. It offers us a counterfeit numbness in return.

Addictions result from unmet needs we don't know we have. Many Christians are addicted to something other than God's genuine love and affection. Socially acceptable addiction such as food, work, and ministry keep us pursuing happiness, instead of enjoying the benefits of R.E.A.L. Joy.

If you're offended by me pointing out your elephant, that's a good indication that shame is at work in your life. Shame is the arch-enemy of joy. It will keep you from *Responding Entirely to the Affections of the Lord*. Most of us have a hard time labeling our "stuff" because we are full of shame, so we hide rather than see it for what it is. Life blindsides us, and the enemy is good at making things look bad.

Remember, I said getting R.E.A.L. would be painful. I know... I have been there. If you give me a chance, I will share my story, and together we will experience R.E.A.L. Joy.

Identify Trinity

The grace of the Lord Jesus Christ and the love of God and the fellowship of the Holy Spirit be with you all. – 2 Corinthians 13:14 *(ESV)*

You may notice that I do not say "The Trinity." First of all, you probably know that the word "Trinity" is not found in scripture; the church began to use the term in the latter part of the fourth century. We use the term "Trinity" to describe the concept of the one God who has three distinct persons: Father, Son Jesus, and Holy Spirit. The more intimate I started to become with the Father, Son and Holy Spirit, the term "God" began to sound too generic and impersonal, as well as saying "The Trinity." So, when I am referring to all three persons of God, I will say "Trinity." It feels like a name versus a title to me. You will notice I also say "Father" and "Holy Spirit" without the word "the" for the same reason. It's kind of like me calling my children "The Kids." It's too impersonal for my taste.

I realize that many are focused on reverence of God and prefer a more formal title when referring to God. Some in reverence will not even write the word, instead, they use "G-d." I mean no disrespect to anyone; I only offer you an explanation as to why I use the name "Trinity" when referring to the three persons of God.

Fire in Ice

It started on a typical Sunday Morning. I was leading the congregation in an activation as our praise band sang in the spirit. They were singing from Psalm 24:3-5; "Who will ascend?" Holy Spirit was leading us to personally experience Psalm 24, so we were letting Him use our imagination to show us how to ascend the mountain of the Lord. I shared that an angel was waiting to take us up the mountain, but that before we could begin, he wanted to examine our hearts to make sure we had clean hands and a pure heart. Each of us pictured ourselves at the foot of the mountain standing with an angel. We asked for our hearts to be examined. It was amazing how powerful God's presence was. He loves to see His children surrendered and willing to yield to whatever He says. After we surrendered and repented for anything unclean, the angel presented each of us with a personalized gift that would help us ascend the mountain. Talking with others afterwards, it was so sweet to hear about the specific things we each saw.

My gift given to me during that encounter was a manual about playing the harp. David used his harp to silence the demons tormenting Saul (1 Samuel 16:23). It is a symbol of how worship is a weapon of spiritual warfare for defeating the enemy. So I asked, "Lord, do you want to teach me more about worship as warfare?" He said, "No, you're going to write this manual." I am presently working on that project and plan to co-write it with a U.S. Marine! Then the angel directed me to follow him. I

> *SURRENDER:*
>
> *Leaning into the change God is initiating instead of resisting it.*

approached another angel who held something in his hand. It was an ice cube with a flame inside of it. The angel said, "You will use this in your book."

I asked, 'What is it?" The angel said, "The fire in ice represents cold love. Those with cold love have conceptions that have limited their passion for God."

"How does this happen?" I asked. "It seems supernatural to have such a perfect balance; the ice isn't cold enough to put out the flame, but the flame isn't hot enough to melt the ice."

"Yes," said the angel, "that is why they think they are being influenced by God to put such limits on Him." The angel told me I would receive the antidote to this problem soon. Then the activation was over.

The Antidote

It was a week later in a conversation with a friend that I received the antidote for cold love. My friend began to share how on the same Sunday at her church, she was also leading the congregation in an activation. Holy Spirit showed her a large rock and told her to have everyone imagine themselves leaning their full weight into the rock. As they were leaning, the rock turned into a large ice cube with a flame inside of it. Wow, God is so cool (no pun intended)! As they continued to lean, the ice started to melt. As it melted, they began to sink into the liquifying ice, and it became refreshing. They further leaned in, surrendering to the renewal, until they reached the flame. In touching the flame, their hearts were set on fire with a greater passion for Jesus. There it was: The antidote is surrendering (leaning into) to the change God is bringing instead of resisting it.'

Surrender is defined as "to cease resistance to an enemy or to submit to their authority." What is it about change that seems like we need to fight it? We all know change is necessary. We can often treat Heavenly Father like He is the enemy when He refuses to protect our way of life. Our human nature likes things to be consistent, convenient, orderly (a biblical term we can use to justify our control issues), predictable and systematic. But, serving the God of the universe can be anything but those things.

> For the invisible things of him from the creation of the world are clearly seen, being understood by the things that are made, even his eternal power and Godhead; so that they are without excuse. – Romans 1:20 (KJV)

I love this passage because we learn from it to use creation (things that are made) to discern what God is like (the invisible things of Him). For instance, we know that God is very artistic and creative by watching a sunset. We know that He likes things to be unique and different by observing snowflakes or the wide variety in every species He has created. Most importantly, we know that God's idea of being consistent does not mean sameness. Orderly does not mean conformity.

How can we learn this through nature? Every one of us in the human race has the same order to the structure of our face. We all have the same number of eyes, ears, nose, mouth and chin; they are all in the same place and yet none of us look exactly alike. Even twins can be recognized with a keener observation. I think that is amazing and tells us a lot about the God we serve.

But my all-time favorite thing I have learned about God through nature is His absolute unwillingness to be predictable! Just ask any weatherman! Yes, God is consistent and unchanging, but it will take us eternity to learn and experience the subtle nuances built into what doesn't change. It's kind of like saying we have seen the ocean because we have stood on its shores. We may think the ocean is pretty consistent from the shore's vantage point, but with every wave that flows consistently to the shore, the ocean is changed. From the shoreline, we can only see the surface of a very small section of the ocean. However, a new vantage point can change our understanding of the ocean: Does it remain the same all the time or not?

Once we realize that we must surrender to a God who is not predictable — who will not conform to our ideas of what is normal, nor will He be limited to our views of theology — then and only then, do we have the chance to start experiencing Him for who He really is. Otherwise, as Paul says, We "have a form of godliness but [we] deny the power thereof" (2 Timothy 3:5). We have cold love. We are fire in ice.

Cold Love

And because iniquity shall be multiplied, the love of the many shall wax cold. - Matthew 24:12 (ASV)

According to Vine's Expository Dictionary of New Testament Words, "iniquity," means unrighteousness. It denotes contempt for divine law. Within the context of this passage in Matthew, Jesus is talking about the culture that will exist at the end of the age. Old love is not caused by the unrighteousness within an individual as much as the contempt for divine law within the culture. If I am a believer in Jesus Christ, my personal sin has been dealt with through the cross. All I have to do is repent when I sin and our Heavenly Father will be faithful and just to forgive me and cleanse me from all my unrighteousness (1 John 5:9). **However, the unrighteousness of our culture can cause our love for God to wax cold, even if we are doing our best to walk uprightly.**

American culture is becoming increasingly rational. We value intelligence and education over morality and Godly values. The emphasis on rational thinking has eliminated communication with God as a valued way to receive wisdom. For example, most people will not argue regarding your right to pray, but if you say that God actually answered you when you spoke to Him, they may argue that you need medication!

Within the church, this cultural iniquity has caused even believers to be skeptical of the supernatural. We rely heavily upon being "realistic" when it comes to faith. A believer who makes a decision to deny rational thinking based on a dream, vision or prophetic word from the Holy Spirit or even the Bible is often ridiculed. Our dependence on rational thinking within the culture has robbed the church of direct communication with God. Our love is waxing cold. We are exchanging faith for common sense and reasoning.

Experiencing Trinity

As believers in Jesus Christ who uphold the doctrines of the Bible, we believe that God is three in one; Father, Son and Holy Spirit. I will not take the time to defend this belief though some will argue it. Yet culturally, many Christians do not even recognize the differences between each member of Trinity, nor do they have a separate relationship with them. The journey to joy begins with getting R.E.A.L. with God. We must know him as He is, not as we imagine Him to be. We can identify

We rely heavily on being "realistic" when it comes to faith. Our love is waxing cold.

and acknowledge each member of Trinity and develop a personal relationship with each of them. So, don't just read this book. Let it take you on an adventure. Trinity wants so much more for you than just an apologetic approach to biblical truths.

As I share, I see myself as a tour guide, not a travel agent. A travel agent will just explain the possibilities; they do not actually experience the places they teach others about. Many approach the Word of God the same way. They read it like a travel magazine, imagining what it was like, but they never go there themselves. The tour guide takes you there. They get you participating. So, I am going to take you into the Word of God to experience the presence of Trinity, creating opportunity for you to hear from each of them for yourself. It will require you to deny rational thinking if you want to go along. You will need to lean into God and totally surrender to the changes that will inevitably come. You will experience your heart being guided by Heavenly Father himself, beyond the edge of Glory where it remains safe. You will experience the limits of rational thinking melting away into a renewal of passion for God. Holy Spirit will breathe life into your tired theology, revealing the glory of God in supernatural ways. Jesus will embrace your heart like a lover, dissolving the limits of your weaknesses and failures. This will require surrender.

Come along on a JOYRIDE with God.

What Do You See?

After attending a gathering of pastors, the following day, an angel appeared to me and took me back to that gathering in the Spirit realm. He asked me what I saw. Looking at the people interacting in the room, I could see insecurity, fear, anxiety, and similar. However, the night before, I had only been aware of my own feelings of insecurity. Now, as I saw in the Spirit, I could see that the atmosphere had been charged with thousands of little electrical bubbles clouding vision and hindering heart to heart contact. Again, our environment and atmosphere drain us, leaving love to wax cold.

The ice was broken (pun intended... remember fire in ice) that night when one of the couples opened up and shared their own brokenness. The angel now showed me what was happening in the atmosphere as this couple began to share. When this couple revealed their hearts, instead of hiding them, it changed the atmosphere. It became filled with a warm glow that melted the resistance between us.

> God is light and in Him there is no deception. If we walk in the light as He is in the light, we have fellowship one with another and the blood of Jesus purifies us from all our sin. –1 John 1:5,7

So often we hide in deception, trying to make ourselves look and feel as good as possible. We are trapped in self-preservation because of past rejection and betrayal. We think that by hiding our true self, fellowship will be easier. We call this deception "wisdom." This is so contrary to Scripture. 1 John makes it clear. In God there is only light or truth. When we are honest and open, we walk in the truth with God.

Unfortunately, for centuries, the Church has demanded perfection, resulting in the world thinking that being a Christian means you believe you are better than everyone else. Most do not even see the cross; the beautiful cross of grace where all my sins are washed away simply because I am honest and confess them, wanting to be cleansed. If we want fellowship with God and others, we must walk in the light, for God is light!

Being R.E.A.L., *Responding Entirely to the Affections of the Lord,* **starts with being honest about how we feel and think on the inside.** We must begin to risk the rejection and come clean with who we really are and how we really feel about things. As long as the Church continues to hide from one another, pretending to be everything we think is being demanded of us, we will have no REAL fellowship with God or others. This deception is rendering the Church power-less to do anything against what is happening in the world. **Getting R.E.A.L. will bring us face to face with our wounds of rejection that have trapped us in the deception of self-preservation that some call wisdom.**

God Is Light

> God is light and in Him there is no deception. If we walk in the light as He is in the light, we have fellowship one with an-other and the blood of Jesus purifies us from all our sin.
> – 1 John 1:5,7

What is light?

Visible light is electromagnetic radiation whose wavelength falls within the range to which the human retina responds — between about 390 nm (violet light) and 740 nm (red). White light consists of a roughly equal mixture of all visible wavelengths, which can be sep-arated to yield the colors of the spectrum, as was first demonstrated conclusively by Isaac Newton. According to *Webster's Dictionary,* the velocity of light in a vacuum is 299,792 km. per second.

Ultraviolet light is having a wavelength shorter than that of the violet end of the visible spectrum but longer than that of X-rays (*Merriam-Webster Dictionary*).

Infrared light is having a wavelength just greater than that of the red end of the visible light spectrum but less than that of microwaves (*Merriam-Webster Dictionary*).

The rainbow is the light that our natural eye can detect, but there is light beyond our ability to see with the natural eye. This light has either a wavelength too short (ultraviolet-beyond the violet on the rainbow) or too long (infrared-beyond the red on the rainbow) for our eye to process.

People who have visions of heaven often speak of seeing colors that are not earthly or part of the rainbow. If we truly want to see God, we must activate the Spirit's eye, which is opened by faith; faith enough to believe that God is all light; far beyond what we can see in the natural realm.

> For we walk by faith, not by sight. – 2 Corinthians 5:7 (*NKJV*)
>
> But the natural man does not receive the things of the Spirit of God, for they are foolishness to him; nor can he know them, because they are spiritually discerned. – 1 Corinthians 2:13-14 (*NKJV*)

The natural man walks by sight, relying more on reason than faith. According to 1 Corinthians, the natural man will not be able to receive the things of God, because they are not based on reason or the visible realm.

> For the invisible things of him from the creation of the world are clearly seen, being understood by the things that are made, even his eternal power and Godhead; so that they are without excuse. – Romans 1:20 (*KJV*)

Romans shows us that the visible realm should not limit our understanding of God, but that the invisible can be understood by the visible. So, we should be able to look at the visible and learn how to see the invisible. In other words, God speaks to us through His creation or visible realm, but in no way should we limit God by the visible or reasonable realm.

> God says, "This is the sign of the covenant I am making between me and you and everything living around you and everyone living after you. I'm putting my rainbow in the clouds, a sign of the covenant between me and the Earth. From now on, when I form a cloud over the Earth and the rainbow appears in the cloud, I'll remember my covenant between me and you and everything living, that never again will flood waters destroy all life." – Genesis 9:12-15 *(MSG)*

The rainbow is more than just a beautiful remembrance that God is good. The rainbow represents all that we can see with the natural eye. Creation is a means for us to see and remember God is good.

Yet, our humanistic culture has chosen to worship creation itself rather than the God who created it (Romans 1:25). We would rather save a whale and protect the earth than honor God by respecting Him as the giver of life. We have elevated woman to the position of life-giver; therefore, our culture believes she has the right to choose.

Humanism, the dominant philosophy of our culture, believes that truth can be communicated through only two ways: reason and experience. All other forms of communication should be suspect. Said plainly, the supernatural realm should not be considered a legitimate means of receiving knowledge. A large portion of our Christian community in America has been influenced by Humanism. They do not accept the supernatural and become suspicious of anyone who does. Instead, they rely on reason, reducing the Living Word of God to reasonable explanation. For example, saying they believe in God, but denying His supernatural power.

On the other hand, Eastern philosophy believes that knowledge can be received in three ways: reason, experience and the supernatural realm, and all three ways are equal in value. This philosophy is one of the reasons why the Christian community in other countries are seeing miracles, signs and wonders. Eastern culture already believes in the supernatural realm. Many of the people have been involved in the demonic realm, so they easily embrace the angelic realm when they get saved. It is easy for them to embrace the true God, who uses His power for their good.

I am convinced that America is being primed for a supernatural move of God that will bring our humanistic culture back to its knees in repentance and acknowledgment of the true and living God and His Son Jesus Christ. I believe that the popularity of the supernatural realm on TV is evidence of this shift in our culture from the total reliance on reason and personal experience to the awareness and acknowledgment of the supernatural. Sure, right now, the TV interest is mainly in the dark side of the spiritual realm. This is because our deeds are evil (John 3:19). But at the same time, God has ignited many in the church to begin to "see" Him beyond the rainbow. We are walking in the supernatural realms with God and He is revealing the mysteries of the Kingdom to us. I personally have visited these realms regularly for many years. However, as a forerunner, for a long time, I ran alone and most of what I could see I was unable to share with others

America is being primed for a supernatural move of God that will bring her to her knees in repentance.

without risking great persecution. But now I am surrounded by many seers and we are all pressing into God, full of passion, pursuing a walk of holiness with Father, Son and Holy Spirit. These are great days to live in!

Yes, darkness and dread threaten us daily, but that is only troubling if you walk by sight. I encourage you to pursue a walk somewhere over the rainbow! God is way bigger and more powerful than we have even begun to comprehend. If we want to experience Trinity as He is, we must let Him use our imagination to take us where our reasoning will never want to go.

So, What Do You See?

Let's go back to my story about the pastors' gathering. Remember I stated that when I was with my friends, I was only mindful of my own feelings of insecurity? It wasn't until the angel took me back to that gathering in a vision that I could see what was happening to all of us. The angel showed me the atmosphere charged with bubbles, making it difficult to see one another clearly. This is representative of a general tendency. We usually judge ourselves based on our intentions, but we judge others based on actions. We can look across the room at individuals who appear to be standoffish and we may assume they are not interested in us. The Lord showed me years ago, that when I felt someone appeared to be ignoring me, more than likely they were feeling like I was; self-conscious and focused on avoiding rejection. Holy Spirit taught me to rise above these fears by directing me to go to those who were alone and make them feel connected. *This is what the Bible calls the Gift of Hospitality, and it is a requirement for all who are called into the ministry!*

When you're in a room of friends, what charges the atmosphere? Is it fear or faith? Insecurity or sonship? Pain or gratitude?

Disappointment or hope? Will you break through the realm of reason to see things as God sees them? You can be the one who shares your brokenness so that others can be healed.

> Walk in the light as He is in the light and you will have fellowship with one another. – 1 John 1:7

R.E.A.L. Joy will require us to stop depending on reason and risk vulnerability. It will require surrender to Trinity, as we open our hearts to each person, Father, Son, and Holy Spirit individually.

R.E.A.L. Joy comes when we Respond Entirely to the Affections of the Lord so we can see things as he does.

So, when you close your eyes to pray, who are you with? Is it Father, Jesus or Holy Spirit? Wait quietly until you become aware of who it is you are with. It may be all three persons; that's when I call them Trinity.

Don't be discouraged if you didn't get it. We are just getting started on this journey. There are several reasons why we may be hindered from this level of intimate connection with God. In the following chapters, we will discover and remove the hindrances as you discover **R.E.A.L. Joy!**

R. E. A. L.
JOY

Let's Get R.E.A.L. with God:
He Is the Source of Joy

Chapter 4

Identify Joy: K.N.O.W. God

For as the heavens are higher than the earth, So are My ways higher
than your ways, And My thoughts than your thoughts.
– Isaiah 55:9 (*NASB*)

I have learned a great deal about God and His nature from several
significant men of the faith; two of them being A.W. Tozer and
Graham Cooke. Throughout this chapter, I will be highlighting
what God has revealed to me through their teachings. I remember
sitting for the first time listening to Graham Cooke. I had been married for four years and was caring for my three small children while
holding the position of associate pastor of counseling in our church.
Safe to say, there was a lot on my plate. Life was crazy.

As soon as Graham began to speak, I felt like I had stepped into a
whirlpool bath for the soul. This man walked in a level of peace I
didn't know existed on earth. At least, none I had ever witnessed.
Most of my mentors at the time were filled with vision, passion, and
fire for God; and when they spoke, they ignited a desire to do something more for God. That was great, but Graham walked in something

different. He wasn't challenging my lifestyle or even my faith; he was challenging my understanding, my experience with what I believed. He talked about the three persons of Trinity like they were friends that he knew well. Holy Spirit had a sense of humor! He told Graham jokes! What?! I thought I had a pretty intimate relationship with God at the time, but I was being introduced to something I had no grid for and I loved it!

I rarely saw a miracle or a manifestation of the Spirit in the many times I heard Graham speak. He wasn't after that. He was encountering God in dimensions beyond the natural realm and invited me on that adventure. Instead of trying to get heaven to come to earth, I found myself simply longing to be in God's world, and He was always willing to take me on an adventure with Him.

I remember an encounter I had during this time of discovery. I was in the darkness and many around me were crying out for help. I was frantically trying to help them, but ahead of me was a bright light. The father kept telling me to come to the light. But I wanted to bring everyone with me. The struggle was so painful. But I finally broke away from the concern in the darkness and stepped into the light. It was overwhelming; sheer joy, peace, love... the pain just melted. All I wanted to do was worship the Lord. As I did, something amazing happened. The light began to spread out over all the people. Pretty soon, everyone was in the light. That encounter changed my life, like so many quiet but powerful moments shared only with Trinity. I was in a different dimension, while everyone around me had no idea what I was experiencing. I was learning at the time that worship could take me places.

I will never forget the first time I saw the Holy Spirit's sense of humor for myself. My family and I were traveling by car in a pretty bad storm. My husband clung tightly to the steering wheel, white-knuckled and quiet. I tried to answer my little children's questions with a happy tone, but I was scared. To myself, I was praying hard for safety. I asked Holy Spirit to protect every tire and to keep the car on the road. The next thing I knew, I was seeing Holy Spirit on the front hood of the car holding an umbrella while soaking wet. He said, "Really; I couldn't help from inside the car?" I smiled and invited him in and He sat next to me, wiping the water off his trench coat and laughing… so was I! The fear left, and I knew we would be safe. Thank you, Graham. You have inspired me to K.N.O.W. God more intimately.

Here's what I know about knowing God…

Knowledge Must Be Revealed.

Head knowledge that is attained by study and not accompanied by experience will only puff you up, making you think you know something because you can behold it intellectually. A.W. Tozer says in his book *The knowledge of the Holy,*[1] "Our creedal statements of belief are of little value compared to our actual thoughts of God." In other words, what I say I believe must match my experience or my words and thoughts will have no power. For instance, I can say I know God loves me unconditionally and quote all the scriptures that tell me so, but if my father left when I was a kid and I am afraid to trust people as a result, my actual thoughts will be filled with doubt. In order for my statement of belief to really be true, I will need God to reveal it to me personally. This is an ongoing process of walking in the Spirit.

Two years ago, I was shopping for a Mother's Day card, and God told me to buy one for myself and consider it from Him. The one

---

1 Tozer, A.W., *The Knowledge of the Holy*, (HarperOne - 2009)

He had me purchase came with a button that He told me to wear on Mother's Day while I was preaching. The button read, "Mother Off Duty." Later that week, during my devotions, I saw myself before the courts of heaven being accused by the enemy of not being a good enough mother. I saw myself holding a stack of tarot cards with the queen on top. I knew I was being attacked by some form of witchcraft. I looked up what that top card meant, and it said, "Mother Smother." The Lord said, "There are several people in your ministry that you are parenting as though they are infants and they are not." He said the enemy was draining me of strength and distracting me. I needed to declare I was a "Mother Off Duty" so that I was no longer under the influence of the accuser of the brethren!

K - Knowledge must be revealed

N- Never be satisfied

O - Open to wonder

W - Withhold nothing

My creedal statement of belief concerning ministry is that I am responsible to people but not for them; Jesus is their Savior, not me. But that statement had no power in my life at that time because I was actually acting as if I were responsible for certain people. Once I repented and got back into alignment, the burden left, and so did the people sent by the enemy to distract me.

My father has always taught me, "What you know can keep you from what you need to know." It takes a lot more than intellectual agreement. We must KNOW the truth for it to set us free. If the promises of God are not working in your life, it's because you need a revelation, not just intellectual knowledge of the truth. Ask Holy Spirit to reveal to you where your actual thoughts are not in alignment with what you say you believe. These imbalances are often buried in memory, and we are unaware of them. Alignment releases power. This is how Holy Spirit comforts us, not by saying, "there, there" and licking our wounds. Instead, He shows us the truth about our situation and gives us an empowering way to think, thus transforming our lives!

Let me give you an example. One of my clients came to me to discuss her broken relationships. She mentioned that she struggled to recover in a relationship once any kind of tension developed. As she allowed Holy Spirit to access her memories, she remembered sitting on the top of the steps as a small child listening to her parents argue. She remembered thinking to herself, "If they really loved each other they wouldn't argue like this." She then invited Jesus into the memory. He appeared to her in the memory and sat on the steps next to her. With his arm around her, He spoke kindly. He said, "People who love each other still fight sometimes." Of course, this woman knew that intellectually, but emotionally she was driven by the lie she decided to believe as a small child... until Jesus healed her that day.

Once, an old childhood friend came to my mind. I remembered how we would play jacks in the school playground after school. But her brother hated me, and I never knew why. The Lord told me I had accepted a lie through this struggle. The lie was, "I am always responsible when someone is in pain and blames me for it." WOW! That was the source of a lot of my shame over the years, because I always assumed I was wrong, no matter what the offense was about. So Holy Spirit asked me to break my agreement with the lie. I spoke out loud, "I choose to no longer believe the lie that I am to blame when someone is in pain." Father spoke the truth and replaced the lie. I then agreed out loud with the truth. Now, I know people in pain lash out but I do not have to accept the blame unless it really is mine.

Holy Spirit comforts us by showing us the truth about our situation and giving us an empowering way to think; thus transforming our lives!

So stop here and ask Holy Spirit to speak to you through your imagination. He may bring to your remembrance a person from your past or a childhood experience. Do not be afraid of these memories or ignore them as if your mind is just wandering. Instead, ask Holy Spirit what He wants to reveal to you about these thoughts or memories in your mind. Let Him show you if you adopted a lie from the memory. Most often, the lie will control our actions subconsciously until it surfaces, and we decide not to believe it.

This reminds me of one of my favorite stories. A little boy wanted to see the parade scheduled to come down his street in a few weeks. It's all he talked about until the day finally came. He got dressed and rushed out the door, but as he did, his mother told him not to leave the yard. That created a problem since the yard had a barricade fence around it. The young boy got a milk crate, positioning it just under the knothole in the fence and stepped up to watch the parade. Even though he could see and hear everything that passed in front of him through the little hole, his vision was limited. Then, suddenly he heard laughter from behind him. He turned to see his older brother on the roof! From above, he could see everything, far and wide with no restrictions. This little story can describe the difference between what we know and see versus how God knows and sees our situation. We will have to leave the knothole and trust God's perspective instead of insisting God look through the hole as though He's missing something.

Knowledge Must Be Revealed

"Thou O Christ, who was tempted in all points like as we are, yet without sin, make us strong to overcome the desire to be wise and to be reputed wise by others as ignorant as ourselves. We turn from our wisdom as well as from our folly and flee to thee, the wisdom of God and the power of God. Amen"[2]

This prayer gets me every time, especially the part about wanting to be considered wise by others as ignorant as ourselves. I don't know whether to laugh or cry at the thought of how true that statement can be. Oh Father, forgive us for the ignorance of our arrogance and for how big we appear to ourselves because our vision of you is so dim! Forgive us for allowing **approval** from our peers, or lack thereof, to blind us from the power of your approval and trust in us! Oh, that we would have dove's eyes as Song of Solomon says. Eyes that see only you with no distraction from the temporal world in our peripheral view!

Never Be Satisfied

"God's wisdom requires that we do not follow our usual pattern, we shall not seek to understand in order that we may believe, but to believe in order that we may understand." [3]

God never changes. At the same time, He opens the possibility for us to become actively involved with His Kingdom. God does not grow, mature or learn anything that changes Him. He does not allow what others do or what happens to change Him. Yet when dealing with humanity, God chooses to partner with us, knowing full well

---

2 A.W. Tozer, *The Knowledge of the Holy,* p. 59
3 Ibid., p. 59

the limitations that come with that. He allows us access to Him, and we affect His sovereignty on the earth.

Let's look closely at Ezekiel chapter 1. In this passage, Ezekiel is having an encounter or activation, as we would call it today. In this vision, he sees a specific type of creature flying around the throne of God. This creature has four heads, the face of a man, lion, ox and eagle. The scripture states that two interlocking wheels covered with eyes flew beneath these creatures. In fact, the scripture says the Spirit of the Lord is in the creature and the spirit of the creature is in the wheels, so where the creature went so did the wheels!

One day many years ago, I was asking Father where the four personality temperaments were in scripture. There are many different tests out there to describe our personality, many of them helpful. But, I knew they had to be in scripture, too; the information is just too beneficial and accurate not to be. He answered my question with this passage in Ezekiel. The four faces are the four temperaments of human nature. The wheels represent the sovereignty of God, moving in all directions at once and covered with eyes, meaning He is everywhere and knows and sees all. The four temperaments each have an expression of God's Spirit. How we see and understand God and move in faith with him affects how His sovereignty moves on the earth. WOW! Why do we struggle with trusting the sovereign God when He trusts us in this way?

God in His sovereignty chooses to partner with frail humanity, but it is by no means an indication of our power over God in any way. He is always in charge, even though He gives us control over certain things.

He even remains true to Himself when dealing with the devil! That is why the devil can act unlawfully if we allow him to. God gave us control over the earth in the garden and we gave it to Satan. Only we can take it back, by applying the power of our salvation through Jesus Christ. God knows all and is unaffected by any of it. Instead, His plans are based on that foreknowledge (Romans 8:29). In this way, we can change and our situations can change, but God never changes! We must hold in tension the equal though seemingly paradoxical truths of God's full sovereignty and our free will when it comes to partnering with God. As the line of one of my favorite worship songs states, "You don't change Your mind and You won't mess with mine, Oh how faithful you are" ("Faithful", by Perry Chickonoski). Sorry, you won't find that song on Google — not yet; my son wrote it!

God has given us His authority to exercise according to our level of faith. Therefore, if we become satisfied with our current level of faith and knowledge, then we limit the sovereignty of God to such smallness. Of course, these limitations do allow the devil to win a few battles. I love what Graham Cooke says about this, "God in His wisdom will prevent what He can easily do with His power." Winning is not the goal for God because He always wins! He created us for relationship, and that requires us to choose Him. That is how important our free will is to the sovereign God. So, while God remains the same, change is consistently altering our perspective of God. The second we think we understand God and how He does something, we prevent ourselves from learning more. Paul says it like this in 2 Corinthians 5:13, "For if we are beside ourselves, it is for God; if we are of sound mind, it is for you." In other words, what we know about God is for the benefit of others; we speak with a sound mind when sharing what we already know about God to someone else. However, when speaking with God, we must remain beside ourselves, in astonishment, perplexed and in need of understanding.

What we know can only serve to help others, but for us it often becomes a wall that limits God in our lives. His Word is true, but our understanding of it grows with our relationship with Him. You cannot confine the Omnipotent Creator of the universe to a book, much less your understanding of it! To do so defies the very essence of what the Bible teaches us about God. God contains the Bible; the Bible does not contain God. **It takes an intimate relationship with Trinity to do what the Word says, "...rightly divide the word of truth" (2 Timothy 2:15). Therefore, we cannot, must not, ever be satisfied with what we think we know about God.** We must have passion, relentlessly pursuing the heart of God. This passion comes not through our intellect but through our experiences and encounters with Him, which leads to more revelation.

Graham Cooke talks about the seasons in which God reveals Himself. He creates the passion within us through seasons of manifestation and hiddenness. The times of hiddenness when we cannot see God at work, often called dry seasons, are meant to drive us deeper into the things of God — much like the root of a plant is driven deeper in search of water. This dryness actually causes the plant to grow stronger, as deep roots keep it steady in the wind. The seasons of manifestation, when we feel alive spiritually, are a time to celebrate the growth that took place in hiddenness — much like spring is a celebration of the growth that took place beneath the wintery surface. When I no longer felt abandoned by God or fearful I was drifting, then hiddenness became precious and more was accomplished in less time. Manifestation came more quickly as I learned to never be satisfied with what I had learned in the prior seasons. God is amazing! He is always lavishing His love on us in undeniable ways if we are looking for it.

I am always looking. As a result, I see God all the time. Several years ago, I came across an article by David Van Koevering called, "Keys to taking your Quantum Leap." David set me on a journey of discovering God at work through quantum physics. Scripture teaches that in the end times, the knowledge of God's glory will cover the earth (Habakkuk 2:14) His glory has always been on the earth, but through quantum physics, He is revealing how His glory works and the knowledge of His glory is being revealed. I had the privilege of knowing David Van Koevering personally after that, and he imparted to me a passion to know the dimensions of faith that go way beyond understanding.

Recently, David went home to be with the Lord and Father saw it fit to give me a portion of his anointing to carry on and impart onto others. For all of you who have kept the faith and fought and failed then picked yourself up over and over again, your struggle is not in vain. David left the earth, as so many have, having not seen in the earth all that he saw by faith. But others and I will carry it on. **Remember, your faith is the substance, the proof, that what we see in the invisible realm is real.** It's not about getting results. We are in a relay race. Carry your baton as far and as well as you can and then pass it on. We are guaranteed to win… together! R.E.A.L. Joy comes in the discovery of who God is. **Never be satisfied with what you know of Trinity!**

Open to Wonder

So we are learning how to K.N.O.W. God for R.E.A.L. Joy comes in the knowing. We are learning:

Knowledge must be Revealed,

Never be satisfied,

Open to Wonder,

Withhold Nothing.

"He is everywhere while He is nowhere, for 'Where' has to do with matter and space and God is independent of both. He is unaffected by time or motion, is wholly self-dependent and owes nothing to the worlds His hands have made."[4]

Remember, your faith is the substance, the proof, that what we see in the invisible realm is real.

While sitting in a worship service one Sunday, Jesus came to me as a Lion. He was huge, and He invited me to crawl up on His mane. I was the size of a gnat clinging to a single strand of hair on His mane. He soared through the heavens and took me up to planets. Then, we flew over what looked like a field of wheat. The wind that stirred by His motion blew on the wheat, causing it to fold over on itself. I clung to the Lion as He kept soaring into the heavens. When He stopped, we were looking down on the field of wheat suspended in the universe. He spoke, "That is time. I am neither in time nor independent of it," meaning God created time separate from Himself, yet He chooses to be a part of it as He wills. I saw that each stalk of wheat represented times and seasons. They were independent of each other and yet also as one as they moved and flowed into each other by the very wind of God.

David Van Koevering taught me that heaven is not *elsewhere*. It's not on the far side of Pluto completely disconnected from our world. Jesus said, "The Kingdom of heaven is at hand" (Matthew 3:2). Quantum physics is explaining what God's Word has been proclaiming. According to David Van Koevering, Heaven is else-when. It is right here, but moving faster than the speed of light, so we cannot see it! Science would call that a dimension.

---

4 A.W. Tozer, *The Knowledge of the Holy, Tozer,* p. 27

Our world operates in time and space. There are three dimensions of space: width, height, length. Everything seen is measured by these dimensions, but when you add the dimension of faith to our world, it changes what we can see. When you add the dimensions of the gifts of the Holy Spirit, these additional dimensions change what we can see. If you try to explain faith to someone who has not opened his/her heart to faith, it will sound foolish to him/her. They cannot see what you see with the added dimension of faith.

In the same way, a believer in Christ who has faith in the true God sees differently than a person who has faith in something else. However, a Spirit-filled believer has dimensions that a faith-filled believer does not have access to, and this also prevents sight. We must open our hearts to the wonder of God. He functions outside of time and space. **When we limit what we see and understand of God to our world, it drastically distorts what God is really like and how powerful we as true believers in Jesus Christ really are.** Remember my story of the little boy and the parade? The parade is there; what you see of it depends on your position. Are you seeing God through the knothole in the fence or from the rooftop?

When my children were in grade school, I got a hernia. I was believing God for a healing. One day while in prayer, the Lord said, "You will be healed when you can see the cardinal in the tree." I didn't know what that meant, but I kept my heart open to wonder and, I waited. I thought, *Well, maybe it will be Christmastime because cardinals in the winter trees are a symbol of Christmas.* But, Christmas came and went, yet there was no healing. I had gotten my children involved, teaching them to see God and have faith. They would always point out when they saw a cardinal anywhere. "Maybe today I will be healed," I thought every time I saw one. I learned during that time that the male cardinal is the bright red one. This color is designed to distract any prey from getting to the female cardinal. Father said, "Your hernia is symbolic of a hole in your spirit. You do not see Me protecting you. When you see My heart to protect you, you will be healed." Ah, the cardinal in the tree!

Finally, the Lord said, "I want you to schedule surgery and believe that you will be healed beforehand." So I did, telling my surgeon what I was believing for. He, of course, told me that would never happen. But I did have several good conversations with him about the Lord. I began thinking this was all for the doctor's faith. Shortly before surgery, I was driving to the office one day, and five cardinals were walking, yes, WALKING across the street! I rarely break for birds since they usually fly off in time. As my car drew closer, the birds just kept walking. I slammed on the breaks. The car stopped. As I watched those five cardinals walk, Father said, "My grace and protection (the number 5 means grace) needs to bring you to a stop!" I realized that I was trying to produce this healing just to prove something to myself, the doctor, and anyone who didn't have the faith I did! Father said, "Your faith is in *your* faith, not in *Me*. I want you to trust Me to take care of you whether you are healed miraculously or I choose to partner with the doctor." *Ok, Father, I will keep my heart open to wonder and not limit You.* I did have the surgery, and my heart was at rest, which healed the hernia of ingratitude in my spirit! That doctor recently died at a young age. I believe God used me to impart faith to him — the kind of faith that keeps believing though not seeing!

The carnal mind wages war against the Spirit. - Romans 8:7

"The natural man is a sinner because and only because he challenges God's selfhood in relation to his own. In all else he may willingly accept the sovereignty of God; in his own life he rejects it. For him, God's dominion ends where his begins." [5]

No one says it quite like Tozer. God's dominion ends where the carnal or natural mind begins. If you need Trinity to make sense to your natural mind and in the natural world of time and space, you will only know *of* Him but not be intimate *with* Him. I believe our culture has reduced a relationship with

Ok, Father;
I will keep my
heart open to
wonder.

Father to that of Judge; Jesus, as the friend who gets you out of trouble; and Holy Spirit, as a force that does crazy things that can't be trusted, and is not relevant anyway. You don't want to be one of those crazy people who swing from chandeliers, right? The church is weak and irrelevant as a result of our carnal theology.

If we want R.E.A.L. Joy in our lives that doesn't fade when our desires are quenched, then we must stay **Open to Wonder.** It cannot and will not make sense in the natural realm; we must receive the added dimensions to see. God is far beyond our thoughts. It's so fun when He gives you a glimpse of what is possible with Him.

Let me share about one of those possibilities with God. One day several of the ladies on our prayer team were praying about a situation, and we were asking for wisdom to see beyond our own understanding. We needed it. The situation was grave. In the Spirit, I saw us inside a large white room that was so bright I could see nothing but the brilliant light. I had the sense that we were inside of God's thought concerning the situation. A portal appeared in the middle of the room, and we were asked to step into it. It shot us up like an elevator, and suddenly we were standing on the outside of a very large

5 A.W. Tozer, *The Knowledge of the Holy, Tozer,* p. 29

white sphere. I then realized that we were in the universe standing on a star. I was overwhelmed with the thought that space is the mind of God and every star a thought! I love when God just shows me stuff that makes me wonder! It brings such peace, joy, and power when we actually experience Him.

We all know God is big, but when He allows us to encounter Him, we change. Please don't settle for what you know. Remain **Open to Wonder.**

Withhold Nothing

Many through the centuries have declared themselves unable to believe in the "wisdom" of God in a world wherein so much appears to be so wrong. However, the Christian view of life is altogether more realistic than human reason. It states that, for the moment, this is not the best of all possible worlds but rather one lying under the shadow of a huge calamity: the fall of man. The whole of creation groans under the mighty shock of this fall. The writers of scripture make no attempt to supply sufficient reason for God's wisdom. They assert that the creature was made subject to vanity, not willingly, but by reason of him who hath subjected the same in hope (Romans 8:20).[6]

Ok, so Tozer gets a little lofty. Let's break this down. We have all heard the argument, "How can a loving God allow such bad things to happen?" I love Graham Cooke's insight into this question. "God in His wisdom will prevent what he could easily do with His power." Most people want God to show up and show off when they want something done, but they totally expect God's wisdom and intervention

---

6 A.W. Tozer, *The Knowledge of the Holy, Tozer,* p. 61

to look a lot like how they would do it if they had His power! The human race can be arrogant largely because we see God so small and human-like, allowing us to see ourselves as more important than we really are. After learning Graham's thought on God's wisdom, I started looking more for God's wisdom than His power. When God didn't do what I expected, I refused to feel abandoned or rejected. I wasn't going to allow the disappointment or even grief to keep me from seeing what God was seeing in my situation. Now that is R.E.A.L. power!

God allowed the Fall to give man a choice, otherwise, we would do as expected. But to give us choice meant He had to create something other than Him to choose, which is evil. We can choose God or choose our own way. Evil continues because man is arrogant and chooses it over God more often than not.

I figure most of you reading this book wouldn't put yourself at this level of arrogance. However, remember my bubble story and how the atmosphere is charged with the feelings and intentions of those around us. The atmosphere of arrogance, in America especially, affects us more than most realize. I am amazed at how easily good Christians who love Jesus blatantly disobey the Word of God with seemingly no remorse, only excuses. This saddens me; we have the potential to be so powerful.

> He has shown you, oh man, what is good; and what the Lord requires of you. Do justly, love mercy and walk humbly with your God. – Micah 6:8

So, let's talk about Hope Deferred...

This is probably a bigger problem to most strong Christians than arrogance. Hope deferred can cause even the strongest of Christians to hide from God, withholding our hearts for fear of greater disappointment.

Hope deferred can be seen in those in need of a healing. Though this is not always the case, I know several strong Christians who choose to accept illness, because they cannot risk the disappointment of another failed prayer.

> Hope deferred makes the heart sick, but a longing fulfilled is a tree of life. – Proverbs 13:12 (*NIV*)

The word *deferred* means prolonged, drawn out, delayed. It also means to submit or turn over to another. It is a challenge, to say the very least, to keep believing for something over a long period of time. This is especially true when the desired results are directly affecting one's own life and abilities. I remember being in prayer for a close family member who was in great physical pain. He had been believing for healing for several years — and continues to believe — for total healing as I write this book. In prayer I asked Jesus, "How is he supposed to trust you and not feel abandoned by you?" Jesus replied, "I don't know; the pain of the cross caused me to ask Father why He had forsaken me." One thing for sure is that we will never know the depth of pain and abandonment Jesus carried for us. For the Father will never turn away from us, as He did Jesus. The pain that sin caused Father, caused Him to look away from Jesus in His most desperate moment.

The greatest testing of our faith is time. Imagine how sick the Father's heart must be as He waits for the world to be redeemed! Consider Jesus. Did He really have to come to earth as an infant, waiting 33 years to do what He came to do? Every moment must have been a struggle for God Himself to have to be human, to even need His diapers changed! Did He have to go that far for us and wait that long? The Bible says that the road is narrow and few find it. Talk about hope deferred! After everything Trinity has done for us, few people will accept its benefit. Father will have to watch His own children choose hell when He gave His only Son for them. Jesus will have suffered in

When I am tired and afraid because of hope deferred, I will give my heart and defer it to God, remembering I cannot suffer for Him.

vain in their lives. And don't forget what Holy Spirit endures for us. He is hardly acknowledged at all in church. He is relegated to a back room for the strange group of "prayer warriors" that are called to that stuff. God forbid Holy Spirit to be allowed to be Himself at church! Yes, time is the greatest test of Faith, but not just ours! Remember, we have a chance with God because He took a chance on us! However long we wait, God waits longer; whatever cost we pay, He paid higher.

He hasn't asked anything of us that He didn't first do Himself on our behalf. We don't deserve anything God does for us; He deserves everything we can do for His sake. We don't understand the *why* most of the time. We see dimly and we prophesy in part, according to 1 Corinthians 13.

This is what I do know. When asked how to pray, Jesus gave these instructions:

Our Father who art in heaven — That puts Him and His ways beyond the natural realm.

Hallowed be Thy name — First thing you do is remember who's boss.

Thy Kingdom come — Pray for His authority to come to earth.

Thy will be done — This is the biggest prayer need.

On earth as it is in heaven — Faith sees what heaven is doing. The battle is to get that same thing to happen here. Just because earth doesn't see it, doesn't mean God isn't doing it.

Jesus goes on to say we need to pray for three things that can be taken from you in the battle, if you pray for the first part of the prayer.

Give us this day our daily bread — Satan steals resources when you're in this battle for the kingdom.

Forgive us our debt as we forgive our debtors — Relationship with God and others will be challenged if we enter this battle for the kingdom to come to earth.

Lead us not into temptation, but deliver us from evil — Jesus knew it could get ugly and the devil would be good at making God look bad. Our situation can even make it look like God is the one who set us up to fail. *First, He tells me to do something and then it doesn't work?* Our faith can seemingly fail, making us look like the idiot, when we were just trying to have faith. Sound familiar? This is the ongoing battle that rages. **Humanity controls the first heaven, God controls the third heaven and Satan controls the second heaven (Daniel 10:13-21, Ephesians 6, James 4:7). It is our job to shift the atmosphere of the first heaven with godly behaviors. Our behaviors are like troops on the ground for the war.** Our prayers and our worship are the air force for this battle; they give us airpower to shift the second heaven where Satan is preventing the Kingdom of God from having authority in the earth.

When I first stepped out in faith and submitted my calling as a prophet to my leadership at the time, they were all for it... in private. But when people started questioning what I was doing and pastors started to argue about the theology of "personal prophecy" and "deliverance ministries," they denied me publicly and allowed the community to believe I was an unsubmissive, self-appointed heretic. It was painful to say the least. One night I sat crying with my husband, telling him that I didn't think I could take all this anymore; it had been going on for years. I was beginning to question if I was even called to be a prophet and if God even still had prophets. While I was sharing the pain with my husband, the phone rang. It was a woman who had confronted me months before. She was a satanist and a witch and had told me she was assigned to take me out. For months she would show up at our services to heckle me as I spoke, until one of our ushers escorted her out of the building. When I answered the phone, she said, "So you don't want to be a prophet anymore?" She actually heard my conversation with my husband in the spirit realm. "OH, IT'S ON!," was my reply. That was an arrogant and fatal mistake on her part and the devil's! If the devil wanted to stop me that bad, it was real for sure. I never looked back again after that!

As hard as that season was, I am so grateful for it. I grew so much in my gifts and in intimacy with the Lord through "hope deferred." Rick Joyner saved my life with his idea about rejection. I enlarged his statement and taped it to my desk; it stayed there for several years. Here is what I learned from Rick: Three things can destroy ministry faster than anything else; self-seeking, self-promotion and self-preservation. Rejection, when embraced as coming from the Lord, will cause us to grow in grace and love. If we do not embrace the rejection, it can lead us into witchcraft.

It was very hard to keep my accusers on the same team. I knew I could not allow the enemy to cause me to go to war with them, instead of him. Ephesians 6 is clear; we do not wrestle with flesh and blood, but with the devil and his demons. This is war. We will win, regardless of how many battles are lost. That's what makes us more than conquerors (Romans 8:37).

So, here is what I have decided to do about "hope deferred." When I am tired and afraid because of delay, I will give my hurt and defer (submit) it to God, remembering I cannot suffer more than He has for me. **I want to be one of the few, the proud, the godly marines, who make it all worth God's efforts.** I will *withhold nothing.*

To K.N.O.W. God
will result in

R.E.A.L. *Joy*
Responding Entirely to the Affections of the Lord

*K - Knowledge must
be revealed*

N - Never be satisfied

O - Open to wonder

W - Withhold nothing

Chapter 5

Activate Joy: Let God Use Your Imagination

I pray that the eyes of your heart may be enlightened in order that you may know the hope to which He has called you, the riches of His glorious inheritance in His holy people, and His incomparably great power for us who believe. - Ephesians 1:8 (*NIV*)

The Eyes of Your Heart

You may have read the book, *School of the Seer*, by Jonathan Welton, so you understand that we have more than five senses. For those who have not had the pleasure, it's a great read. We have 15 senses in all. The same five senses we have for our body, we also have for our soul and spirit. Here are a few examples:

The phrase "I smell something fishy" is not referring to a physical smell, but an emotional one. Our soul is discerning or "smelling", that something deceptive may be going on with people in the room.

Another example, "I can feel you're up to something" is again not physical touch but our soul's sense of touch.

In this passage in Ephesians, Paul is referring to our spirit's ability to see, when he says, "I pray the eyes of your heart may be enlightened." So how does our spirit see? The Bible refers to this ability as visions, dreams, and even trances. A vision is a dream when you are fully awake. A trance is a vision so intense that you can feel the physical sensations as though it were actually happening in the physical realm. A trance involves all the senses at times. Paul was experiencing a trance when he said he wasn't sure if it was in the body or out of the body (2 Corinthians 12:2). It was so intense he wasn't sure if he was actually transported like Philip experienced. Philip was taken up in the Spirit and relocated to a different city to minister (Acts 8:26-40). These things happened frequently in scripture, something that most Christians are too carnal to expect to happen today, yet Paul prays that we experience these things so we can know our calling, have unity with the body of Christ and walk in God's power. Dreams, visions and trances all take place through our imagination. Our Children's Director is teaching our little ones to have "faith eyes." We do this by allowing Holy Spirit to sanctify our imagination.

> *Dreams, visions and trances; all forms of biblical communication; all take place in our imagination.*

Of course, the enemy has his counterfeits to all of this because that's what he does. If the world has a counterfeit, then rest assured that God has the original, and it belongs to us. We must redeem these things instead of throwing the baby out with the bath water. Fortune-telling is the counterfeit to genuine prophecy; tarot cards and crystal balls counterfeit the seer gift. Drugs can be sorcery, a form of witchcraft. In fact, the root word for pharmacy is "pharmakeia," (NT Greek) which means sorcery in Greek. The devil uses our imagination as his playground, causing addictions, depression, fear, anxiety, etc., and all too often we let him do as he wills with our minds and imagination. Yet, at the same time, we have been convinced that God doesn't use our imagination or our emotions, so we limit God's intervention in this area, giving free rein to the devil. For example, I firmly believe that many who are addicted to porn really have a strong seer's gift, and the enemy is stealing that gift and perverting it. It is time for us to take back the truths and starve the enemy's counterfeits.

> But solid food is for full-grown men, *even* those who by reason of use have their senses exercised to discern good and evil. – Hebrews 5:14 (*ESV*)

One develops into a mature believer by using their senses to discern good (what God is up to) and evil (what Satan is up to). Romans 12 tells us that whatever gift we have, we must use it according to our level of faith. That means you will get better in discerning God and what He is doing by using your gifts and risking failure. You must have the mindset of training, not trying. A good athlete doesn't quit when the game is lost. Instead, he figures out what went wrong and fixes it. When you train, you learn by using your gift until you perfect it. Unfortunately, the Church has not been a good coach when it comes to the development of spiritual gifts. We expect perfection, and when someone fails, we judge their character. Instead, we should be coaching them to get better at their gift! Just another way the devil manages the power of the Church!

> God does not give us a spirit of fear (timidity), but of power and of love and of a sound mind. – 2 Timothy 1:7 (*NKJV*)

Many Christians make the fatal mistake of thinking fear or discomfort is discernment. But this scripture is clear — God does

not speak to us through fear. When we are afraid or uncomfortable with something or someone, we must submit our fear to God first (James 4:7). Then God can speak to us. When God speaks, even if the natural response is to be afraid, we won't be. We will have love, power and a sound mind instead.

A closer look at the word fear in this passage can be translated as "timidity" (a feeling of disapproval). God is not the one making us feel rejected, shamed or guilty; that comes from the enemy; the one referred to in Revelation as "the accuser of the brethren" (Revelation 12:10).

If you're going to see into the spirit and mature in the spiritual gifts, it will take risk and a willingness to fail in order to get better. Find a fellowship that celebrates the risk and coaches believers to become full-grown, able to discern good and evil. It is a journey towards maturity but the joy of the Lord will be your strength. Like all good fathers, Heavenly Father is a great coach and loves to see us try.

Yearly Themes from God

Since my freshman year of college, every August, the Lord has given me a theme for the year. I received my first theme in August of 1985. I just assumed the Lord was sticking with the school calendar; however, it wasn't until 2010 that I learned about the Hebrew calendar (the Hebrew New Year begins in September). Without knowing it, I have been on God's calendar. I love how God does things! He is not limited by our limitations. We can partner with Him without understanding if we just listen and obey!

So, in 2010, the Lord told me I was entering the Decade of the Seer. Honestly, I thought I already was a seer, but wow, did I have a lot to learn. This journey has been amazing! Each year, along with a theme,

I also receive a symbol. The symbol for the first year of Decade of the Seer was the blue butterfly (which later became the symbol for our ministry). This butterfly is blue at the top of its wings and camouflaged on the bottom. It takes concentration and patience to see the blue butterfly in motion. It flashes blue then it's gone. You can't grasp it or keep it unless the life is gone out of it. Then you can frame it in a little box and put it on display. This is what it is like to see God. You must quiet yourself, watching and waiting just to get a glimpse. When you do, it's exhilarating! However, you cannot grasp God. The second you think you have Him figured out, the life in your relationship is gone. He's been put in your little box to display. In 2010, we noticed the blue butterfly everywhere. Christmas decorations were all about blue butterflies. They were on T-shirts, jewelry, advertisements and even commercials.

One such experience was during my son's school field trip to the zoo. We were greeted by a giant banner filled with blue butterflies advertising the new blue butterfly exhibit! My son, who was in eighth grade at the time, insisted that one of the blue butterflies would land on me while in the exhibit.

> *You cannot grasp God; the second you think you have, the life in your relationship is gone.*

I went in, agreeing with his faith. But after about 20 minutes, I knew we had to leave and catch up with the rest of our group. We were standing in line to exit, and my son was still full of faith. By this time, I was praying the disappointment wouldn't damage his child-like faith too much. We were next in line to leave the building, and the exit process included two sets of doors with a large corridor between. A group of us filed through the first set of doors, and they closed the doors behind us and paused to make sure no butterflies exited with us before they opened the outside doors. They were about to release us when I noticed a blue butterfly perched on the back of the man in front of me. I spoke up, motioning to the exhibit worker not to open the doors. She then told me to gently pinch the wings together and carry it back inside. I was dumbfounded. My son, full of faith, was beaming. I did what I was told and gently set the blue butterfly on my hand once I got inside. It opened its wings fully and sat in my hand as my son and I gazed in delight. Then, it was gone. God is amazing. He is at work all around us! All we have to do is give Him our imagination. He will give us "faith eyes" in return. **There is no greater joy than seeing God! That's why Paul prays that the eyes of our heart will be enlightened.** Yes, it takes risk and your willingness to fail, but just one glimpse of God's majesty makes it all worth it.

Who's in Charge?

Sometimes, we have to make a choice about who is in charge of our imagination. Scripture tells us to be anxious for nothing (Philippians 4:6). Anxiety starts in the imagination. We speculate what might happen. We have conversations in our heads, imagining what we would say if certain situations played out in the natural. We hear a sound and imagine a burglar is breaking in. Our child is past curfew and we imagine a police officer knocking on the door to give us the bad news. Over time this consistent use of fear driving our imagination creates a state of anxiety, but we have a choice! We do not have to let fear control our imagination.

We have to make a choice regarding who is in charge of our imagination. Anxiety starts there as well, speculating what might happen.

Years ago, very dear friends of my brother were killed in a plane crash while on vacation, leaving a new baby back home. My brother was filled with anxiety at the thought of what it might have been like. He was imagining their terror and regret at the realization that they were going to die. But I said to him, "If we are going to speculate what happened as the plane was going down, let's use faith instead of fear. Let's imagine that they were filled with the Holy Spirit, stood up and started preaching the gospel assuring the salvation of everyone on that plane."

> But, he said to me, "My grace is sufficient for you, for my power is made perfect in weakness. Therefore I will boast all the more gladly about my weaknesses." – 2 Corinthians 12:9 (*NIV*)

God's grace is sufficient. We have all we need for what we are going through. However, we do not have grace for what we imagine. How many times have you been at a funeral thinking, *What if this were me?* When we are imagining a terror, we have no grace in it. However, in real darkness, God's grace, love, and peace sustain us. It benefits us in no way to give our imagination over to fear. We have the power to determine who is in charge of our imagination. If you're going to speculate about the outcome, let God be in charge of what you are imagining.

Fear makes us weak; **not faith!** God is an ever-present help in time of need. Worry has no preventative quality. In fact, the power of our intentions are creative. The power of life and death is in the tongue (Proverbs 18:21) and the tongue speaks from the imagination; what you imagine has the power to create. Now, this is not an exact science because our battle is in bringing heaven to earth. Even though this does not always work, that doesn't mean it's wrong. Our faith is the evidence of what we hope for, not the desired outcome.

In quantum physics, this power is called "popping a quiff." Here is a quick science lesson, as I *understand* it. Everything invisible is a wave and everything visible is a particle. Science says a wave must be observed in order to become a particle. When this happens, we pop a quiff. Something must be observed in its wave state for it to become visible. Of course, science takes the position that it doesn't know who the observer is. Really? We know from scripture that God spoke everything into existence. The wave of His voice turns everything into a particle. I love this! Scripture tells us that our faith is the substance (particle) of things not seen (wave). So when we partner with God through faith to see the unseen, we turn it into something visible. Science is finally catching up with the Bible!

In 2011 the symbol I received was a banana, and I thought for sure *that* wasn't going to be around as much as when it was the blue butterfly. Sure enough... it was! It felt as though the banana industry was exploding that year! For instance, I walked into my daughter's basketball game that fall and paper bananas were decorating the hallways of the opponents' school! You can't make this stuff up! So crazy how much fun it is to see God and join him!

By the way, the banana was the symbol because the Lord told me science would become significant that year. The banana is a symbol for Intelligent Design theory that has the potential to eliminate the theory of evolution! 2011 was the year I met David Van Koevering and began to study quantum physics. More on that later. **God is specific, not illusive, if we are looking with faith eyes.**

The theme God gave me for the year 2014 was "Maximize Royalty" and the symbol was the peacock. Needless to say, Christmas decorations were all peacocks and they were everywhere that year. The morning the Lord was speaking to me about the year's theme, I was on my back deck for hours researching the peacock. I discovered amazing things that helped me understand the significance of this symbol. For instance, peacocks can eat poison and not die; their feathers are covered in eyes, which makes them a symbol of both wisdom and pride. There is a fine but crucial line between an arrogant mindset and a royal one. When I finished studying, I joined my kids in the kitchen. As we were talking, something caught my eye running swiftly through my yard. You guessed it... a peacock. They, of course, are not indigenous to Ohio! It disappeared into the woods before I could get my kids to see it. They just laughed, thinking their mom was having one of her crazy visions again, but it was so real looking. Two weeks later, the headlines in our local newspaper read, "Strange Peacock sightings on Clingan Road." The peacock had gotten loose from a nearby farm, but the timing made it a supernatural experience.

God loves to set things up for us to see Him all around us! It just takes faith and our imagination! *Activate joy by giving God your imagination.*

Chapter 6

Release Joy: Trust God in the Pain, Disappointment and Rejection of Life

I sat weeping as though I was experiencing what I was watching on TV. Then I heard God say, "You have experienced this." I was watching the end of a series about the development of America. The series ended with two women as the only ones left of an entire caravan of wagons. This caravan had headed out to California from the east coast. It had consisted of many pioneers full of dreams just two years prior, but now these two women stood alone among hand-made wooden crosses in a field. They marked the graves of their husbands and children. They were alone. No family. No dream. All was lost. One woman said to the other, "We have lost everything for nothing." They turned away from the camera to walk off into the distance and disappeared. But the viewer knows the rest of the story! They lost everything, but not for nothing! Americans went west. The dream thrived. We are living it!

Believer, this is your honor, your calling, your hope. Lift up your eyes to the hills from where your help comes. The dreams we share

for our world are eternal. **They will take many lifetimes to ful-fill! This is a relay race. We run our leg to the best of our abilities through faith and pass the baton to the next generation. Your sac-rifice may be great, but the reward will be greater.** Run the race as Jesus did. He is the author and finisher of our faith. He gives us R.E.A.L. Joy - the joy of the Lord is our strength.

How Did Jesus Have Joy?

Looking unto Jesus the author and finisher of our faith, who for the joy that was set before Him endured the cross, despising the shame, and is set down at the right hand of the throne of God. – Hebrews 12:2 (*KJV*)

This is the new covenant promise. If we keep our eyes on Jesus, which means we see him as the author and finisher of our faith, we will have joy. Joy which enables us to endure suffering while despis-ing the shame of it. Once we do this, we will receive our reward as Jesus received his.

So, here are the boundaries and benefits of our covenant with Jesus:

1. **Jesus is the author and finisher of our faith.** We must trust Him to know more than we do when things are tough. The devil is good at making God look bad. If we take our eyes off Jesus, we move out-side the safe boundary of our covenant. We are on our own until we decide to look at Jesus and not our situation.

2. **Jesus carried His cross to victory.** There is a beginning and ending to our cross. Scripture teaches that the light and momentary afflictions of this life cannot even be compared to the eternal weight of Glory that we share with Jesus (2 Corinthians 4:17). We must know the times and seasons or we will carry a cross past the point of resurrection.

3. **Jesus embraced the cross and despised its shame.** We often do the exact opposite. We despise the cross and endure the shame. Joy cannot be found in our trials this way. We are called to count every trial as joy (James 1:2).

4. **Jesus' intimate knowledge of Father as rewarder, not punisher, gave Him unstoppable joy.** Hebrews 11:6 states, "It is impossible to please God without faith, for we must believe that He is and that He is a reward of those who diligently seek Him." There are absolute truths that must remain the foundation for how we process all that we learn and experience in God. Knowing that God is a rewarder, not a punisher, is one of those absolute truths that must govern the way we see and experience all of life, not just through the things that bring pleasure. It often takes faith to see God as a rewarder because life makes it feel like we are being punished. Human nature has a tendency to only see what we have concluded as true. Once we decide something to be true, our brains shut off and we are unable to keep processing the information. This is why we must learn to walk by faith and not sight. God is always working to reward us; we must not shut our minds off too soon, or we will fail to see what is really happening. If you choose to believe you are being punished, that is what you will see. We must believe that He is a rewarder in order to see the reward in our situation! That is how Jesus kept His eye on the joy that was before Him. He was utterly convinced the cross was a reward because His Father is a rewarder of those who diligently seek Him.

Let's explore each of these more in depth:

The Boundaries and Benefits of Our Covenant

1. Jesus is the author and finisher of our faith.

Our faith starts with a promise. When Trinity created Adam and Eve, they released the hope and dream for every person to be born from them. Genesis 1:1 says, "And God saw that it was good." Creation was an idea in the mind of the eternal God. When He spoke, He saw His idea fulfilled. Revelation 3:20 says, "Behold, I stand at the door and knock." He still waits for us to answer the door. The covenant cannot be put into action unless we want it to. We must keep our eyes on Jesus. When we take our eyes off Jesus to look at our situation, the flow of covenant is cut off. Covenant is still there, but we put a crimp in it by looking away. Peter experienced this when he was walking on the water. As long as he looked at Jesus, He was fine. The second he looked away, down he went. The same happens to us.

I experienced this in my approach to healing. I used to be so focused on trying to get people healed instead of looking at Jesus, the healer. Father kept saying to me, "Stop trying to produce healing; you need to learn to receive it." We can learn this lesson through the life of Joseph, Jacob's son. I have studied Joseph's life over the years. One night at a party, I was asked a question, "If you could spend one day with any influential person dead or alive, who would it be and why?"

> *Father said, "Stop trying to produce healing. You need to learn to receive it."*

The person asking the question said, "I know we would all want to be with Jesus, so for the sake of variety, choose someone else." I knew immediately it would be Joseph. When asked why, I replied, "He was able to stay faithful and did not lose his trust in God despite the many failures, disappointments and rejections. I would love to know what sustained him."

The following day while spending time with Trinity, I went into a trance. In today's language, we say activation. Remember, this is when we are in a dream while fully awake and our senses are fully involved. It feels as though what we are experiencing in our mind's eye is actually happening. Most Christians have had encounters with God where you know He has spoken, there is no doubt. We called these encounters "Wow experiences" in the eighties. We have been praying for revival and asking for heaven to come to earth, so now, our experiences are more than a momentary encounter. Now we are being escorted into the heavenly dimensions. Jesus said, "The Kingdom of heaven is at hand." It is nothing to be afraid of or skeptical of. Trust God to lead you!

So, in this activation I was taken into a beautiful Victorian-style room. Holy Spirit told me this room was the receiving room and I was to wait for my guest. While waiting, my eyes noticed a beautiful fountain, so I moved closer to see it better. As I stood admiring this fountain, I heard a voice behind me and saw Joseph sitting on the sofa. He said, "So, I hear you want to talk with me." Blown away that he heard me the night before, I sat down and he began to speak.

Let me pause for a moment. I am not a medium; I do not summon the dead and they do not speak through me to anyone. Necromancy, the practice of summoning the dead, is forbidden in Scripture and is the devil's counterfeit. However, God on several occasions, sent someone who was dead to speak to another who was alive. Saul tried to use the Witch of Endor to summon Samuel after his death (1 Samuel 28). But God sent the actual Samuel, and the witch was scared to death! I love that! Satan tries to counterfeit God's power, but the witch knew the difference between her power of necromancy (which the Bible forbids) and God's ability to send Samuel. Also, on the Mount of Transfiguration, Father sent Elijah and Moses to speak to Jesus while Peter, James, and John experienced this encounter. Remember, Jesus is the author and finisher of our faith. We do not control it; God does!

So Trinity sent Joseph to me…so precious and personal to my faith! Joseph spoke, saying, "Faith is a magnifier. Whatever you direct it toward will be magnified. If you direct your faith towards cancer, you will magnify cancer and it will appear larger than God. But if you direct your faith toward God, He will always be larger than your situation." He then shared with me that the prison was his secret place with God. It was a blank slate that kept him from being distracted by the cares of life. The cave was a habitation for the presence of God. From there, God took him all over the world to experience what God saw and He prepared him for what would happen when he got released. Then in my activation, Joseph and I were taken to Egypt. He was sitting on the throne where he later served. Joseph said, "When I finally got here (the throne of Egypt) God would often take me back to the cave in my quiet time, to remind me of who I was and who He was."

Wow! This changed my entire perspective on healing. I no longer made it my goal to get people healed. I wanted us all to see God more clearly to discern His heart and plan. Joseph helped me move closer to Jesus by teaching me how to keep my eyes on Him. Jesus only did what He saw His father doing (John 5:19). His focus wasn't on seeing people healed, but seeing what His father was doing and joining Him there.

What are you focused on? Are you looking to see what Jesus wants to do in your situation or are you trying to get Jesus to see what you want to be done in the situation? Our eyes must be on Jesus, the author and finisher of our faith. **God speaks with a promise but it takes time for that promise to be made manifest in the earth. We need to wait on God without getting disappointed or disillusioned (Isaiah 40:31).**

If you are raised with Christ, seek those things that are from above...
set your mind on things above and not on things from earth. –
Colossian 3:1-2.

Sometimes we are believing for a wish, not a promise. A promise
originates out of the mind and heart of God with an eternal purpose.
A wish originates out of the human mind with a temporary purpose.
We must learn to set our minds on the promise sent from above, not
on a wish that originates from below. Navigating the difference can
be tricky. Our human nature struggles to see the eternal value in
pain. We want to wish it away but then feel abandoned by God when
He does not perform our wish. He has many promises in scripture,
but He controls the who, what and where of those promises, not us.
It is our job to keep our eyes on Jesus and learn to trust Trinity so
that we can see what They are doing to perform Their promises!

Signs from Heaven

Let me share my journey through this process with you. Ten years
ago, I began to have several dreams over a three-month period that
my prayer partner was going to die. At first, I thought nothing of it.
Often, when you dream of someone, they do not represent themselves, but rather have symbolic meaning in your dream. I was asking God if there was something important to me that He wanted
me to let go of or give to Him. I wasn't getting any answers. Then
several other people shared that they had dreamed that Marie died…
hmmm? I shared with Trinity that I was not ready for that even
though I was getting a strong sense this was true. So strong that I
envisioned her releasing prayers from heaven for me. The thought
of losing Marie prematurely saddened me, but at the same time I
started to get excited about the possibilities. I was excited, thinking
she would be joining the great cloud of witnesses watching our race.

I asked, "Ok, if this is true, can you allow Marie to send me a single white rose (her favorite) from heaven as a sign that she made it and all is as we have believed?"

The next Sunday, I walked into the room where the eleven of us met to pray and fast. Remember, we had left on our Abrahamic Journey already. Marie, who receives roses from the Lord often, handed me an article from *The Reader's Digest* to show me her latest one. The article, titled "From Above," grabbed my attention because it had a single white rose in the corner. I took the article and started reading. It was about a man dying of cancer whose wife asked him on his deathbed to send her a white rose as a sign that he made it to heaven safely. The man died, and the article went on to share how she in fact got the white rose from her husband.

I started thinking, "God, this is too strange, and I'm a little freaked out." Seeking my husband's wisdom and covering, I explained everything I'd been experiencing. He started laughing and said, "Only Marie would get to go to heaven, bring you back a rose as a sign that everything is true, and not have to die to do it!" That was it! More than ten years later, Marie is alive and well. Thank you, Jesus!

The next week Marie and I shared with the group what had happened. At the end of the worship time, I was caught up in the Spirit and saw Jesus standing with an older woman dressed like a nun. He leaned over and said, "So do you think she believes us now, Theresa?" Ok, now that blew my theology right out the window again. God is always showing us things beyond our limited understanding of theology. We have finite minds and need Holy Spirit to guide us into all truth. Holy Spirit went to great lengths to communicate His message in a very real way. It was amazing to tell the story to everyone who had a dream about Marie.

You might be asking, so what's with the nun? Well, I come from a Catholic background and still have strong born-again family members who are Catholic. One such relative is my cousin Elizabeth Ficocelli, a well- known catholic author and radio host. Around 18 months before my Marie and the rose encounter, Elizabeth had finished her first book and gave me a copy to read. The book was titled, *Therese, Faustina, and Bernadette,* and it was about Saint Teresa of Avila.

Her story is that she was a strong believer with a healing anointing and asked the Father if she could maintain a healing ministry in the earth after her death. The book was filled with testimonies of people who were believing Jesus to heal them and as they prayed, they received a rose letting them know that Saint Teresa was believing with them for their healing. The book gave all the praise to Jesus, not the saint.

I was intrigued, to say the least, especially since, as you already know, my prayer partner Marie receives roses from Jesus all the time. So I told the Lord, if this is actually true, and you have allowed this woman to still have a ministry, then I want one too! It can't hurt to ask! I then asked if He would let Teresa send me a rose in a way that would be undeniable, so that I would know it was something He permitted her to do. Believe me when I say, I had totally forgotten all about the book about Saint Teresa and asking for a rose from heaven. I had no memory of it, until I saw Jesus with Teresa when it was all over! Trinity releases R.E.A.L. Joy, when we learn to **R**espond **E**ntirely to the **A**ffections of the Lord. Now please do not form a new theology about this stuff, I am sharing my story, not creating doctrine to live by.

Trinity releases R.E.A.L. Joy when we Respond Entirely to the Affections of the Lord.

But wait, there's more. Now fast forward about four years after I received the rose. My sister-in-law had just lost her mother to cancer on Mother's Day. After the service, I went to the store to buy food, like a good Italian woman, and headed to my brother's house. While in the store, I spotted a red tulip plant and thought of Betty (my sister-in-law). I walked into her house and presented her with the red tulip plant, saying, "These are especially for you." She broke down crying and couldn't even speak. My mother and sisters surrounded her, but we didn't know why the plant brought such a response. Finally, she was able to tell us. She had asked her mother to send her a red tulip as a sign that she was in heaven. She had not told anyone so she would know it was a God thing. Just to confirm the evidence, the next day she got a card with a red tulip and a blue butterfly (our symbol) on it. The card read, "Your mother loved you… and from heaven loves you still." God is amazing! When you keep your eyes on Him, you see His promises fulfilled even when your wishes aren't. So, the first boundary and benefit of our covenant with God is: ***Keep your eyes on Jesus, the author and finisher of our faith.***

2. Jesus carried His cross to victory.

The scripture teaches us that we must pick up our cross and carry it in order to be a disciple of Christ. Even Jesus dropped His cross several times because of its sheer weight, but resurrection did come. We must expect a cross *and* we must expect a resurrection as well! If we only have a cross and no victory, the covenant has been breached!

Earlier, we discussed how to practice using our senses for discerning good and evil. If we are not mature in this area, we can miss the new season and keep carrying a cross that God is not asking us to carry anymore.

Consider Abraham's ups and downs in trying to discern the voice of God. He had sold out his own wife in fear instead of trusting God (Genesis 13). So when God told him to sacrifice his son, He was going to obey (Genesis 22). Imagine for a minute how his self-talk might have gone: *I will obey God. I don't understand it, but I have learned the hard way that I cannot question Him.* All the way up that mountain, the agony, despair and fear were probably unbearable. The worst part — Sarah had not heard God's command. Sarah did not have a good track record trusting God's commands. She had laughed at the angel who told her she was having a child (Genesis 18:12). What was she going to do when He told her this! Ever been in a scary situation like this? You know God is speaking, but you can see a world of heartache coming out of it. How could this be God? It is in these moments that we must carry the cross. Even if we fall under the weight of it, we must trust God to keep us going. This is not the time to take our eyes off Jesus and do our own thing. The devil is so good at telling us what it will cost us to obey God, but he never tells us what the cost is for disobeying. That cost is always greater.

So, Abraham gets to the top of the mountain. His son is asking all kinds of questions. He lifts His hand to obey God...then he hears, "Stop!" I don't know about you, but sometimes I wonder if I would have just said, "I rebuke you, Satan; I know what God told me to do!" and down would have gone the knife! But thank God Abraham had his eyes on God and could discern His voice and shift into obedience.

Are you discerning the shifting of God's voice as He maneuvers you through the minefield of life? In one season, He may tell you to do one thing and then in the next season tell you to stop doing it. People can easily miss the hand of God directing them — mainly when they have not yielded complete control to Him. The relationship with God is our responsibility, but the direction belongs to Holy Spirit. He is the one showing you what truth in God's word applies to each situation. The Bible tells us to turn the other cheek and it also says dust your feet off and move on. Holy Spirit is the one who guides us into all truth (John 16:13). He is the one who makes us good stewards rightly dividing the word of truth (2 Timothy 2:15). It is imperative that we have a relationship with Father, Jesus and Holy Spirit. Some, however, only have a relationship with Trinity's Book, and refuse to believe that Trinity desires relationship and still speaks to us today. This is so dangerous for mere humans to be navigating God's Truth without Him.

We all have a cross and a victory. Make sure you are carrying the cross God has asked you to carry and not someone else's. Just as important, make sure you put down your cross and walk into victory when God says to stop. It takes a deeply intimate relationship with each person of Trinity to effectively carry our cross to victory.

Meekness and purity are essential to the development of intimacy with God. To carry our cross to victory requires the kind of intimacy that can hear God and obey what He says, no matter the cost. Meekness enables us to hear God when He is saying something that differs from our own ideas and desires. However, meekness is often associated with being mild-mannered or weak; this is not desirable to most. But meekness, as presented in scripture, is not weak. **Meekness is a complete surrender to the goodness of God, and that takes strength.**

Song of Solomon 4:4 describes the meekness of the Bride, "Your neck is as beautiful as the tower of David, jeweled with the shields of a thousand heroes." The neck in scripture is symbolic of our will. The tower of David was the tower at the end of the city wall where all the warriors hung their weapons during a time of peace. If they were at war, the tower would be empty. Jesus is describing the will of

His Bride who is at total peace with God. There is no war in her. She is not fighting for her own way. She is meek, totally surrendered to the goodness of God.

No matter what is happening in our lives, the goodness of God can never be on trial. If we are not surrendered with full assurance that God is good, then our hearts will build a case against God and will never be able to trust His judgments. If we cannot trust God, we will never carry our cross to victory. We will end up despising our cross and using it to justify our disobedience. We will believe our cross creates an exception to God's judgments, saying things like, "God doesn't expect me to forgive when I have suffered such abuse," or "I can't possibly tithe until God gives me a better job."

Matthew 5 states that the meek will inherit the earth. I want to use quantum physics again to relate meekness to the quantum description of gravity. Imagine four people holding out the four corners of a blanket and dropping a bowling ball in the middle of it. The weight of the ball would pull down on the blanket. Therefore, anything of lesser weight when dropped on to the blanket would roll towards the bowling ball. This is how gravity works. Space is like the blanket and the earth is the bowling ball. Everything gravitates towards earth because of its weight.[7] Likewise, when we surrender to God's goodness, which means never warring with him about what is happening, then our faith carries more weight than our situation. The situation then remains within our control. But if we surrender to our situation and go to war with God, our situation carries more weight and we get sucked into it. The meek, those totally surrendered to the goodness of God, inherit the earth. When the Bride becomes arrayed with meekness, the earth will come under our control; not the other way around.

---

7 Einstein, Albert, *The Theory of Relativity*, 1915

The pure in heart see God (Matthew 5:8). The NT Greek word for "pure" *katharos* means to be pruned like a vine in order to bear more fruit. It also means to be purified by fire. We know that scripture teaches us that God prunes us like a vine and cleanses us like gold in the fire (John 15:5-6; 1 Peter 1:7-17). Holy Spirit often uses our cross as a part of the purification process. If we do not trust that God has our best interest in mind, we can end up prolonging the process. God in His mercy never lets us fail one of His tests. We just take them over and over until we get the right answer. The goal in pruning or purifying our lives is so we can see God and have a more intimate relationship with Him. It's not because we are a disappointment and need to be punished. Meekness helps us stay engaged in the process so we can see God and all His beauty in every situation. This is how we become more than conquerors. We win, even when unpleasant things happen, because meekness and purity allow us to see God. He is always beautiful and pleasant and will comfort and strengthen us with His beautiful version of our life. This is how Jesus carried His cross to victory. He had his eye on the joy that was before him; He accepted His Father's beautiful version of His life.

So what is the difference between pruning and purifying our hearts? A vine is pruned when a perfectly good branch is cut off, so that the remaining branches can bear more fruit. **Sometimes God wants to remove perfectly good things from our lives. It has nothing to do with those things being sinful or wrong. Their season is just over.** We must be meek and fully surrender to this process.

Recently, the Lord challenged me that my season as a personal counselor was coming to an end. It was time for me to turn the leadership of our Unleashed Healing Center over to someone else. I birthed the center, learned the techniques we use personally from Holy Spirit, and trained the staff. They are amazingly anointed. It was time for me to let my baby grow up! None of this is bad for me. I am good at what I do, but the season for it is over. I must allow the Lord to prune this branch in my ministry so that others can advance as well as I did. I am seeing God do amazing things because I have engaged in this process instead of resisting it.

We are also cleansed and made pure through the Refiner's fire. As gold is heated in the fire, the impurities will rise to the surface. The refiner then clears the impurities, leaving pure gold. The refiner knows the gold is cleansed when he can see his reflection in the surface of the melted gold. How does this look practically in our lives? Well, think about this... What comes out of you when the heat is turned up in your life? I wish I could say that scriptures come out of me every time I am in a stressful situation, but that ain't true (slang for emphasis)! Contrary to how others may make us feel in our failure, God fully expects the dirt in our lives and character to rise to the surface when we are under stress. God wants us to learn and grow through failure, but our pride often causes us to ignore or deny our failures so we can look as good as possible. This is similar to little kids playing peek-a-boo. They cover their eyes and think they can't be seen because *they* can't see. Remember, the truth sets us free, but first, we have to see it, face it and admit it.

The goal for many can also be to avoid acting poorly by controlling the situations that would otherwise draw out the dirt. In this way, we remain full of impurities and cannot see God even though we look good at a distance. We must not fear failure or deny that it happens. We cover this in greater detail in the next chapter.

For now, it's important for us to have the mind of Christ when considering our failure. God expects failure; it shows we are trying. Unlike

God expects failure. It shows we are trying. He is not afraid of it; we are.

us, He's not afraid of it. Jesus' blood covers it and all we have to do is lean into the process of purification instead of fighting it. Humility is the willingness to be known for who you are, no more and no less. Pride will manifest through arrogance when we try to present ourselves as better than we are, unable to acknowledge faults and casting blame. Pride equally will manifest through insecurity when we back away and hide because we are unwilling to even risk falling short. God resists the proud but gives grace to the humble (1 Peter 5:5-6). Whether we are arrogant or insecure, the focus is self and not God. Only those who walk humbly with God will be purified, and the pure see God.

When we walk in meekness and purity, we see God. God is then able to direct our steps as we carry our cross and walk into victory over it.

The second boundary and benefit of covenant is that **Jesus carried his cross to victory and if we remain in covenant, we will be victorious as well.**

3. Jesus embraced the cross and despised its shame.

With every cross, there is shame attached to it. In fact, the shame related to our cross may be the pain it causes at times. In all that Jesus endured for us, the physical pain was only part of it. Consider the emotional pain when Jesus said, "My God, My God, why have you forsaken me?" Every cross we have to bear has the potential to make us feel as though we have been abandoned by Father. Also, consider the emotional and spiritual pain Jesus endured because of the smug and arrogant political and religious leaders who had no idea of His strength or their weakness. Their ignorance was fortified by the humility of Jesus and His ability to not have to control them or the situation. Most humans have a very hard time letting others think they are right when we know they are wrong. It takes a great deal of humility and strength to remain quiet in those situations. The endurance of Jesus to embrace His cross is not only amazing but something *we* are all called to do as well. Jesus embraced all of this pain because His eyes were on something else. He was not fixed on the pain; He was looking at the joy ahead of Him.

Jesus promised we would endure pain. He said, "In this life you will have tribulation" (John 16:33). **There is no point in trying to avoid it. In fact, avoidance usually creates and/or prolongs pain.** We cannot avoid pain but we can choose the *type* of pain we will endure.

Productive pain: This is pain that has purpose and will lead to an increase of joy once the purpose is discovered and pursued. Productive pain asks, *What is next and what is this for?*

Non-productive pain: This is pain with no purpose and usually is the result of the pursuit of happiness, comfort or removal of displeasure. Non-productive pain asks, *Why me? Why not someone else?* These questions keep the cycle of pain without pleasure going in our lives.

A cross comes from God. Jesus said that if we did not pick up our cross and carry it, we would not be His disciples. Trinity does use pain to purify us, promote us spiritually, and prepare us to rule with Him in eternity. Now, not all conflict or suffering is a cross, some of it is our own doing and some comes from the enemy. But all pain can become productive, depending on our trust level with God. He will always lead us through the pain to an increase of joy. But that requires embracing the pain to discover and pursue the purpose.

The devil, of course, just wants us to suffer indefinitely. He does this by speaking abandonment into our pain, SO THAT WE

WILL NOT EMBRACE IT. Jesus Himself felt this abandonment on the cross when he said, "My God, My God, why have you forsaken me." However, He regained His focus and released His life into the hands of His loving father. Jesus knows every bit of our pain (Hebrews 4:14-16).

Often we despise the cross and embrace the shame. Satan is great at speaking lies to make us feel shame. Growing up, most of us heard "shame on you" when we did something wrong. Shame does not come from God. Sorry, moms; shaming your kids into doing what you want has little lasting effect. Shame usually builds a lack of integrity. At best, people do the right thing when the right people are watching to avoid shame, but there is no real conviction to do right when no one is watching.

We must follow Jesus and carry our cross like He did. Let me give you an example. I have struggled with my weight most of my life. By the time I was in high school, I weighed 185 lbs. I know I don't have to explain the shame attached to that problem.

We live in a culture that worships an ideal image of a man and woman. We hold up those images and judge all those who do not measure up. In our digital world, this image is invalid, yet we still do this. Why are we so critical of each other and ourselves? Simply put: the curse of sin. Women long for men's attention, but men lord over them instead (Genesis 3). Also, according to Romans 1, when a godly culture denies God's power, as we began to do in the 1960s, we end up worshipping the creature rather than the Creator. When we kicked God out of our government, we replaced Him with humanity, and we have been paying the price ever since.

I spent my early years doing what everyone one else does, trying to meet the standard by losing weight. I embraced all the shame I felt and tried everything to get over it. One day in my late 20s, the Lord said, "This issue is a thorn in your flesh that I am not going to remove so that it develops humility in your life" (2 Corinthians 12:7-10). Not everyone with a weight problem has a thorn in the flesh. This was something personal the Lord was asking me to carry as a cross. He told me I had to stop dieting and learn to love myself as I was. This journey has taught me so much about myself, God, and most importantly, the power shame has to keep us trapped. I have carried my cross, quit trying to lose weight, and I have learned to love myself wholly. I learned to despise the shame.

When we embrace shame, we won't be able to face it, so we fight it instead. We will cast blame and shift our focus to avoid the pain, but only when we despise what shame does can we get free from its trap. Not until I stopped trying to measure up, not until I stopped fighting the shame, did I realize how much *We must despise shame instead of fighting it, so we can recognize its control over us.* self-hatred I carried. I would walk past a mirror and curse myself with horrible self-talk. I was being completely controlled by shame. Jesus was never controlled by shame. He despised shame and recognized its destructive power to weaken His ability to fulfill His destiny. We cannot fulfill destiny without carrying our cross, despising its shame and gaining the victory. So, are you embracing your cross or embracing your shame? Are you walking in productive pain or in non-productive pain? Are you despising the shame or walking in self-hatred and shifting the blame? Will you allow Holy Spirit to show you shame's power in your life?

In order to release joy, you must allow Holy Spirit to reveal purpose in life's disappointment, pain, and rejection. **The third boundary** and benefit of our covenant with God is that Jesus embraced the cross and despised its shame.

4. Jesus knew His Father was a rewarder, not a punisher.

> It is impossible to please God without faith, for we must believe that He is and that He is a rewarder of those who diligently seek Him. – Hebrews 11:6

It takes faith to believe God is who He says He is. Life has a way of distorting how we see God and what we think He sees in us. So, let's talk about quantum faith. The best way to describe faith is to use an example from quantum physics. We have probably all seen a movie in recent years that demonstrates the belief that additional dimensions exist. If we could access these dimensions, our view of the world would change dramatically. One such movie is *Men in Black*. The main characters see the world more accurately and have the ability to keep others from accessing the information they have. I am not advocating that Martians are controlling us, but I am just using this movie as an example of what an added dimension does to perspective. These movies are not merely the imagination of a good playwright. They are based on quantum physics which believes there could be up to 26 different dimensions. Scientists use an analogy called "flat land" to help us see the potential for these dimensions.

First, we know that in addition to time, our world has three dimensions of space (width, length and height). Our world is measured and viewed through these dimensions, but if a world existed without the dimension of height, it would be flat land. Everything would only be measured in length and width, so if something entered this world that had height, no one in flat land would see that object correctly. A house, for instance, would only be seen as a flat square, measuring the width and length only. If you could see the height of the house and tried to explain what you were seeing, everyone else would think you were crazy! So it is with faith. Faith is a dimension that changes what we see. If we try to explain faith to someone who does not see that dimension, they think we are crazy. According to Romans 12, faith has levels. We are instructed in this chapter to use our gifts according to our level (dimension) of faith. This is why even among people of faith there are arguments about what is seen. With every dimension of faith, we gain a new perspective that changes what we see.

> For I'm going to do a brand-new thing. See, I have already begun! Don't you see it? I will make a road through the wilderness of the world for my people to go home, and create rivers for them in the desert. – Isaiah 43:19 (TLB)

It takes a dimension of faith to see the way in the wilderness or the river in the desert. When you see it and start telling people what you see, they will think you're seeing a mirage! **People who do not see God do not have the dimension of faith. They only view life through the three dimensions of space and time.** People who believe in God but think He is a God made in man's image have not seen him. They can discern God is there, beyond the natural dimensions, but they have not seen Him. It is similar to the scientists who have discerned there are dimensions but who would probably never see faith as one of them.

It takes a dimension of faith to see the way in the wilderness or the river in the desert.

Those of faith in the true God see God. He is real and when they talk to Him, He talks back! This is an added dimension; without it, you are blind to most of God's beauty.

Yet there are those who have seen God as a punisher. They have a level or dimension of faith that is immature. They need their faith expanded to a new dimension to see Trinity doing something new. God is all-knowing and eternal. Everything He is, He has always been. Nothing is new to Trinity. The next time someone is telling you about an experience they have had with God that is foreign to you, do not allow fear to control you. Submit to God and ask Him to reveal Himself. Scripture teaches us that a fool is wise in his own eyes, but the wise seeks counsel (Proverbs 12:15). Be careful you're not dismissing God and holding onto your limited theology of Him.

It is our cross, the trials we experience in life, that can be the portals into deeper dimensions of faith and intimacy with Trinity. This is the joy that was set before Jesus. He was seeing and experiencing the cross through the dimensions of faith that brought Him joy. James 1:2-3 teaches us to count our trials as joy, for the testing of our faith is producing patience and when patience has its perfect work, we will lack nothing. The biblical understanding of patience is "keeping your passions at a distance." We must be able to move away from our view on life and the passions it creates in order to have our faith expanded. By allowing our trials to keep our passions at a distance, we will then gain a new dimension of faith, lacking nothing!

The purpose in all trials is to expand our view of God, releasing joy and fulfillment in our lives. It takes faith to believe God is who He says He is. Without faith, we will limit God to our world, making Him so small and human-like! We must also believe that He is a rewarder of those who diligently seek Him. God is not trying to punish us; He is not trying to inflict pain. God is everything good and pleasant. When we believe that God is good and a rewarder even in disappointment, rejection and pain, we open a portal to increase the dimension of faith we walk in and the result is pure joy!

Hebrews 12 describes the boundaries and benefits of our covenant with Trinity. We learn from this chapter how Jesus ran His race, giving us the keys to running ours. When we choose to carry our cross to victory with meekness and purity, our faith sees God as a rewarder, not a punisher. **This empowers us to trust God in our disappointments, pain and rejections of life, releasing R.E.A.L. Joy.**

R. E. A. L.
JOY

Let's Get R.E.A.L. with Self: We Mandate Joy

Chapter 7

Embrace Truth: Surrender Fear; Find Joy

I remember the day the Lord instructed me to ask my pastor if I could preach for two weeks. At that time I was the Associate Pastor of a very traditional Pentecostal church. My pastor trusted me explicitly; we had grown up together. However, females preaching on a Sunday morning only happened when asked, which he seldom did. It was a rarity and usually only happened when my pastor was on vacation. Holy Spirit gave me a message that would require two weeks... really? I needed to ask to preach and expect to get two weeks in a row... Ok?

See, this is the kind of stuff that determines if we live a normal Christian life or a supernatural one! I had a choice, as we all do, to make excuses for holding on to the fear or risk it and see God do something supernatural! It reminds me of the scene in *Indiana Jones and the Last Crusade*. Picture it. Indiana is searching for everlasting life. He is using his "father's book" filled with riddles that will save him from the booby traps! Indiana is in a cave and comes out on the edge of a bottomless crevasse. He can see the opening to the cave on the other side, but there is no way to get there. The riddle in his father's book says, "The leap of faith will save you!" He looks again, and a stick picture of a man stepping off the ledge is in the book! He battles in his mind, "This can't be, but the other riddles proved to be right." He closes his eyes, trusting his father's word and steps off. It made absolutely no sense until he used his faith. When he stepped off, the bridge was there. It was a step below the ledge, but it blended into the rock formation, and it wasn't visible until he stepped onto it! That is a perfect illustration of the supernatural life of faith. If you want to increase your bandwidth (more on that in a minute) and enter greater dimensions of faith, you will have to surrender fear and take the leap! I love it! (If we are watching for it, we can see that God is using Hollywood as much as the devil!)

Surrender Fear

Let's go back to my two-week sermon. I made an appointment to speak with Pastor Tony, and I shared what God had shown me. God had given me two circles side by side and said, "These circles represent the natural world and the spiritual world. One world is yours, and one is Mine. I already came to your world, so you could learn to live in Mine." Holy Spirit shared that we cannot fulfill our destiny if we keep trying to get God to come to our world and do things as we see them. We have to let Holy Spirit lead us into all truth (John 16:13). Truth is in God's world, and if we are going to seek God with all of our hearts, we will have to take the risk and learn to live by the spirit, not the flesh (Romans 7 and 8). When we consider "the flesh," many think of sin, which is a part of it. But Jesus tells us in Luke 9 that we are to deny ourselves. Paul says he dies daily to self, and in Ephesians 4:22-24, he instructs us to put off the old self and put on the new man. We are to receive the mind of Christ (1 Corinthians 2:16). If you want more information about how to die to self, you can read my book *Becoming Lovers: The Journey from Disciple of Christ to Bride of Christ.*

When we are instructed in Romans not to walk in the flesh, it means to not make decisions according to the natural mind that always wages war against the Spirit (Romans 8:7). We have to choose to live according to the Spirit realm accessed by the Holy Spirit or live by the carnal world accessed through the flesh (with all its passions and ideas). Paul asks the question in 1 Corinthians 3:3, "Are you still acting like mere men"? He was referring to their jealousies and futile arguments about the law. When we try to make sense of God's Holy Word without the guidance of Holy Spirit, we reduce it to a set of rules without life.

This message about the two worlds was the two-part series I presented to my pastor in hopes he would let me preach. I told him that God had told me that when I preached this message, revival would break out in our church, and nothing would be the same after that! It was hard to put myself out there, but I did, and so did my pastor! He let me preach for two weeks, and at the end of the second sermon... revival happened! The Holy Spirit came upon those of us that surrendered our flesh and said we wanted to live in God's world, not ours anymore. We started to see manifestations of the Spirit that I had not experienced in a long time. Back when my pastor and I were kids, our parents got saved through the renewal in the Catholic church and we saw all kinds of crazy manifestations, but now that we were "more mature believers"... well, not so much!

We were excited. We knew it was God. We had seen it before. A few weeks later we heard about a revival going on in Brownsville, Florida, and off we went! We knew something amazing was going to happen. God was doing supernatural things, and those who decided

Fear is the threshold into the kingdom of darkness. It doesn't matter if you're afraid for good reason. Fear is not the godly response.

to live in God's world were enjoying it. Those who stayed in the natural world left. They left angry, offended, self-righteous, full of fear and convinced we were all crazy and not following the Word of God. Revival is costly. Following the Spirit is risky. We did make mistakes and we were wrong in some areas, but nothing a little grace, love and Godly council couldn't handle. It's sad we never got any of that. Fear is the threshold into the kingdom of darkness. It doesn't matter if you're afraid for good reason! Fear is not the godly response.

God does not give us a spirit of fear, but of power and of love and of a sound mind. – 2 Timothy 1:7 (*NKJV*)

God does not speak with fear. Fear is not discernment. Just because you're afraid, uneasy or uncomfortable about something doesn't mean that God is warning you to stay away. God does not speak to us through fear; so when God is speaking, there is peace, even though there may be good reason to be afraid. God will give you love, power and a sound mind in every situation. That will absolutely require a surrender of fear first.

The body of Christ is plagued with fear, letting the enemy use our imaginations to conjure up so many fear-based assumptions about God, His children, and even our life. The enemy uses fear to absolutely debilitate and disempower us.

Now, I hear some of you saying, "But Joy, fear is sometimes a good thing." Fear can be a tutor — for example, learning not to touch fire because we are afraid to get burned again. However, our response to the fear should not be fear but wisdom. **Wisdom is teaching my children about the importance of being careful regarding fire when I am afraid they may get burned. If I run around trying to get them to avoid every possibility of getting burned, then I'm being ruled by fear and it's not good wisdom.**

I had someone come into my office once, full of passion for our men. He wanted the men of RLM to be afraid of pornography and its deadly effects. He shouted passionately out of love and concern, (so he thought). "I want them afraid! Afraid they will lose their wives, their families, their jobs!"

I said very calmly, "Not in this ministry." He was stunned. I continued, "We will empower the men to see that they are greater and more significant than what porn is doing to them. We will not use fear to manipulate them. Fear comes from the enemy, and it will not produce what you're desiring." He left puzzled and confused, stating that as a woman I had no real understanding of what men were up against. A few minutes later, he returned to my office, thanking me for the revelation. Listen, there are many things to be afraid of… many. But fear is not going to solve any of these problems! Perfect love casts out all fear, according to the Word of God (1 John 4:18).

The solution is to increase our bandwidth! This is a computer term to most. Very loosely speaking, the bandwidth of a computer determines the amount of information that can be processed in a certain amount of time. If your computer is running slow, you must reduce the data absorbing the bandwidth or pay money to increase the bandwidth. It can be likened to a sink pipe. If the "bandwidth" of the pipe has decreased due to a clog, the clog must be removed or the water will run very slowly and the sink will not drain properly. It is the same with our ability to receive love, power and a sound mind from the Lord. If your ability to receive information from Holy Spirit runs slowly, you need to declutter your mind. For example, meditation on God's Word, worship, and confession to a close friend that will love and challenge you are all great ways to cleanse our minds from the wrong ideas, beliefs, thoughts and feelings that shrink our bandwidth. When making a decision, we must deal with fear first.

Recently, my husband and I were facing a difficult financial decision. We were in an office with a salesman that was giving us strong arguments to make a significant financial commitment, and fear was settling in. I was afraid to not act, and my husband was afraid to do as we were being instructed. There is no way to hear God in this environment! I told the salesman we needed to step outside. He offered to leave, but I knew we needed to be away from the environment in his office. Once we walked out and took a deep breath, we prayed for wisdom. Immediately God gave us a plan that gave us both peace. When fear sets in, deal with that first and trust God for wisdom. Never make fear-based decisions. God does not speak with fear!

People tell me all the time, "I wish God spoke to me like he does you," and I reply, "He does."

Consider the cell phone. The signal being released is picked up by a cell tower that is close by. The sound waves transmitted in the air are available to be picked up by the equipment capable of doing so. We need to develop our ability to be a sound tower for heaven. God is speaking. The question is, "Can you receive the signal?" Fear blocks our reception. If you are a fearful person, then waiting to deal with your underlying fear until you face a fearful situation is not the right time (like in the above example when my husband and I faced a financial decision). If you're fearful, then fear will overwhelm you in that difficult moment and you will not be able to step away from it. In that situation, fear must be recognized as a choice being made because somewhere you have made an agreement that gives fear control.

For instance, in college, I suffered from debilitating panic attacks. If you have ever had one, you know how horrible they are. The standard response is medicine, but God told me I could medicate the symptoms and tolerate fear the rest of my life or I could tolerate the symptoms long enough for God to heal my fear. I chose to find out why I had fear instead of medicating the symptoms, and I am so grateful I did. I discovered several lies I believed that triggered fear and anxiety. Now I can gain the victory over fear instead of being its victim. I am not advocating that anyone on medication should stop without consulting their doctors, but while on them, seek God as to why you suffer from fear and anxiety. Do not accept the prognosis that it's just a physical ailment, and therefore, you have to tolerate it the rest of your life. Let God show you the lies, get free, and perhaps you will be able to stop the medication someday. **Surrender fear. Increase your bandwidth so you can receive what God is saying.**

Just for fun, if you have a smartphone, turn it over. Chances are you are looking at an apple with a bite out of it. We are walking around all day long with complete access to the Tree of the Knowledge of Good and Evil, but we need to be eating from the Tree of life instead! Choose wisely what you put into your minds. It is either increasing or clogging your bandwidth to hear God.

Embrace Truth

One of the most quoted scriptures is, "The truth will set you free" (John 8:32). But in the words of Inigo Montoya, "I do not think it means what you think it means." The whole truth about this scripture is that it says if you know (intimately understand) the truth, it sets you free. That is much more than memorizing the written Word. Jesus said to the Jews who had believed him, "If you abide in my word, you are truly my disciples, and you will know the truth, and the truth will set you free" (John 8: 31-32).

"Abide" does not mean "know my word." And a disciple is not someone who goes to church on Sundays and does more good than bad in the name of Jesus. "Abide" (Gr. *menō*) means "to be as one, to not become different, to wait for, to continue with." John chapter one refers to Jesus as being "The Word." Jesus refers to himself as the way and truth and life (John 14:6). He is the Word and the Truth that we must abide in, be one with, wait for, continue with, even when the going gets tough; even when our flesh is crying out in a dry and barren place. If I know Jesus and trust Him at His word, He will set me free.

No one likes to learn that they are wrong or falling short. We all see the blind spot in others. We say things to ourselves (and sometimes others) such as, *Why does he let his wife talk to him like that?* or *Wow, what's with that outfit? She looks horrible.* Unfortunately, few believe they have a blind spot others can see. That is why the Bible tells us there is wisdom in counsel and a fool is wise in his own eyes (Proverbs 19:20; 12:15). At Real Living Ministries, we have adopted a few phrases to help us embrace truth:

1. **You will rise no higher than your actual thoughts about God.** Our creedal statements are of little value, so be honest about what you're really feeling.

2. **What you know can keep you from what you need to know.**

3. **Our brains do not have the capacity to tell us that the information we have stored could be wrong.**

These truths are honored in our ministry. We agree to allow the people we love and who love us to remind us of them when truth is hard to hear.

The worst thing to be afraid of is the Truth. Jesus is the Truth. I know we have all been hit hard by self-righteous criticism that has made us a little gun-shy. I am not suggesting that we make ourselves vulnerable to just anyone; however, we must be vulnerable to someone, preferably several, for more protection. Again, the Word says,

We must choose to respond to the affections of God and others, not to the accusations of the enemy.

> Confess [our] sins one to another that [we] might be healed.
> –James 5:16

I regularly submit myself to those on our staff. I invite them to speak into my life, telling me what they see. We have cultivated a culture at RLM that does not fear feedback. We are worshippers in truth. When you embrace truth instead of avoiding it, the result is **R.E.A.L. Joy**. I am learning to **Respond Entirely to the Affections of the Lord** by responding to the affections of our amazing team. Pastor Judy is one of them. She reminds us of the advantages of accountability. She urges us to remember the person's heart during confrontation. The enemy is always right there in conflict, bringing accusations against God, ourselves, and others. We must make the choice to respond to the affections and not the accusations.

> Faithful are the wounds of a friend. – Proverbs 27:6 *(ESV)*

Jesus is Truth, so we cannot embrace Jesus without embracing truth. The four boundaries and benefits of covenant with Jesus take on new dimensions as it relates to embracing truth.

> Therefore, since we are surrounded by such a great cloud of witness-
> es, let us throw off everything that hinders and the sin that so easily
> entangles. And let us run with perseverance the race marked out for
> us, fixing our eyes on Jesus, the pioneer and perfecter of faith. For
> the joy set before him he endured the cross, scorning its shame, and
> sat down at the right hand of the throne of God. Consider him who
> endured such opposition from sinners, so that you will not grow weary
> and lose heart. – Hebrews 12:1-3 (*NIV*)

The word *therefore* points to the previous chapter to gain more clarity about the cloud of witnesses. Hebrews 11 is affectionately referred to as "The Hall of Faith." It provides testimonies of saints who have gone on before us. Most of those honored never saw the promises fulfilled in their lifetime. Remember my example of the movie I watched about western expansion? It's like a relay race that is costly, but not for nothing. We must draw daily encouragement from Hebrews 11 by those who have already finished their leg of the race. The word *surrounded* means "to be held in a boundary by." This cloud of witnesses serves as our boundary and benefit of our Covenant with God.

Why is embracing truth important? In the natural world, we are daily surrounded by those who oppose truth. Through media, arts and entertainment we are bombarded with images and messages. Our bodies and minds are responding to the beat, usually without acknowledgment. However, we can choose to reject their arguments. I call this influence the enemy's cloud of witnesses! At times, it's so easy to be surrounded by this cloud, held in a boundary that suffocates R.E.A.L. Joy. It's so hard to oppose the opposers.

To protect ourselves, we hide in the church pew and defend the truth without upholding it. We are scared of the big bad wolves. We get angry at anyone who tries to breach the walls. Don't let them in or they will destroy us. What has happened to the glorious church of Jesus Christ? Fear rules, and grace is only for those who act like us. We understand our own sin but cannot handle someone else's. We risk little. We obey when it makes sense, but most of all, we will not be vulnerable to anyone. Never let them see you sweat!

So sad, we are missing out on love, power and a sound mind. **If we are going to have R.E.A.L. Joy, we must be surrounded by God's cloud of witnesses. We must surrender fear, increase our bandwidth to hear God, choose to walk in the Spirit and embrace Truth as a person, Jesus Christ!**

Then we can cast off the weight and the sin that so easily entangles us. The word *weight* (Gr. *ogkosa*) in Hebrews means "something causing drag, holding you back, a burden, mindset, or weight that is hindering you." The word *glory* (Gr. *kabod*) means "weight, the heaviness of God's authority manifesting in our lives." In addition to Satan's counterfeit of the cloud of witnesses, he has a counterfeit glory that we must cast off. Anything that comes from the mind of Satan like fear, jealousy, rage, unforgiveness, hate, envy, gossip, condemnation, self-righteousness, pride, etc. is counterfeit glory. They are intellectual commodities of the enemy. He surrounds us with his cloud of witnesses. He tries to get us to make a bad trade by walking in his counterfeit glory. It weighs us down and buries us in defeat. Don't trade God's glory for a counterfeit. It is time to cast off the counterfeit glory of the enemy and walk away from his dark cloud of witnesses that keeps us in defeat. Come on, Bride of Christ! Arise! Do not be entangled in the affairs of everyday life but be a good soldier (2 Timothy 2:4). Keep your eyes on Jesus, the author and finisher of your glorious faith. There is a race marked out for you in victory!

The word *entangle* (Gr. *euperistatos*) means "to skillfully surround; to prevent or retard running (like an opponent would cut off another runner)." Saint, Child of the Living God, you are the Bride of Christ, a son of God, you are glorious! Satan is trying to cut you off from your race, your purpose, your destiny. Lay aside the weight and the sin that has so easily entangled you and run! Run hard, fast and straight into the loving arms of Truth. Let Him embrace you. Truth will set you free!

Find Joy

There are lots of good, godly definitions for joy out there. My favorite acronym is **J**esus first, **O**thers second, **Y**ourself last. But the working definition for this book and my life is *contentment in the will of God*. When we have fully surrendered our fear and have embraced His truth, there isn't much left to rattle. Contentment is the result of **R**esponding **E**ntirely to the **A**ffections of the **L**ord. I mean, deep, lasting contentment even in the face of life's challenges, people who hurt us and pain that grips us. It's not about being happy all the time. Pain can steal happiness but not joy that comes from a life of surrender. I love what A.W. Tozer says about joy; "Joy is the comfort and delight of the indwelling Spirit which will often spring up like a well of water in the desert, not because you have sought it but have sought rather to do the will of God at any price."

Jesus says it like this, "If you seek to save your own life you will lose it, but if you give up your life for the gospel you will find it" (Matthew 16:25). Fear is having an agenda other than God's. But when I have fully surrendered my fear, I have no agenda but God's. I enter the place of rest where I am free from having to have my own way. I can rest in God with full assurance that He has my back, knowing what is best. Though I walk through the valley of death, I fear no evil! That is a safe place to be, but you must face every fear you have to get there!

R.E.A.L. Joy, contentment in the will of God, is a process that is well-defined by the Shulamite woman's journey in Song of Solomon.

Fear is having an agenda other than God's.

Surrender Zone #1. "My beloved is mine and I am His" (2:16): First, she surrenders her heart but not her will. She accepts a partnership with God and states that her beloved belongs to her first. Then she belongs to Him. In other words, She is still in charge and she will consult God when she needs to. This is the level where many remain. They maintain a personal agenda trying by their good works to get God to agree with them.

Surrender Zone #2. "I am my beloved's and He is mine" (6:3): She has surrendered her control in the relationship now; she belongs to God first. She is learning to trust God and what He wants instead of trying to get Him to see things her way. Greater joy is entering her life as a result. She knows God needs to be in charge and wants Him to be, but she still maintains some ideas she is hoping God agrees with. Many in this zone pray for what they want and then add at the end, "Lord, Your will be done." They are too afraid to ask if what they want is His will or not. They choose to maintain the hope that their agenda is God's.

Surrender Zone #3. "I am my beloved's and His desire is for me" (7:3): Here she has finally surrendered her will and no longer has her own agenda. She is content, full of joy, knowing that whatever God allows into her life, pleasant or challenging, His desire is for her! She knows He is good and has something good for her in everything. She is not afraid to seek His will, allowing God to show her His heart, so He can change hers. That is the place of rest.

The ultimate place God has designed us to live is in freedom — freedom from fear, sin, unhappiness. "It is for freedom's sake that Christ came. Do not allow anyone to place you back under a yoke of slavery" (Galatians 5:1). Fear, our personal agenda, keeps us in bondage. As we struggle to get our own way, the weight becomes too heavy to bear. Surrender to the goodness of God (meekness). It sets us free from fear and we find joy.

Freedom Gauge: Determine Your Capacity for Joy

A+ Freedom: I love doing what is right.

Put off, concerning your former conduct, the old man which grows corrupt according to the deceitful lusts, and be renewed in the spirit of your mind, and that you put on the new man which was created according to God, in true righteousness and holiness – Ephesians 4:22-24 (NKJV)

B+ Responsibility: I do what is right, because I love God.

No soldier in active service gets entangled in the affairs of civilian life; so that he may please the one who enlisted him to serve. – 2 Timothy 2:4

C Obedience: I do what is right, 'cause it's right, but I hate it sometimes.

For I delight in the law of God according to the inward man. But I see another law in my members, warring against the law of my mind, and bringing me into captivity to the law of sin which is in my members. O wretched man that I am! Who will deliver me from this body of death? – Romans 7:22-24 (NKJV)

D– Guilt: I want to do what is right; I just can't change.

Christ purchased our freedom and redeemed us from the curse of the Law and its condemnation by becoming a curse for us. – Galatians 3:13 (AMP)

F Bondage: I am fine; I don't need anyone telling me what to do.

And this is the condemnation, that the light has come into the world, and men loved darkness rather than light, because their deeds were evil. – John 3:19 (NKJV)

You will notice with the **Freedom Gauge** that obedience is a starting point for freedom. Living a life of obedience, as described on the freedom gauge, is an average life; it's not the abundant life Jesus died for, so that you might have it. Jesus came for freedom's sake, not obedience or even responsibility (see gauge). He wants us experiencing the fullness of joy. This happens when we allow God to take us through the surrender zones to complete joy.

> You make known to me the path of life; in your presence there is fullness of joy; at your right hand are pleasures forevermore. - Psalms 16:11 (*ESV*)

I know beyond a shadow of a doubt that I have been put on this planet to release the joy of the Lord. It is my name and my destiny. I am to unleash Father's true thoughts towards His people. He is in a good mood! He is not a joy-killer. He is not as nearly worked-up about the state of affairs as most of His children. God knows all and it's all working into His plan. **The journey is the destiny for God. It is all about revelation. He longs to reveal the hidden mysteries of His heart and plan to you, so sit and rest awhile. Father's heart is joyful, hopeful, and at ease with you. Come along, I will show you.**

In the summer of 2008, we went to Las Vegas on a family vacation with my husband's sister and her family. I wasn't exactly thrilled about going to Las Vegas with our kids until the Lord showed me I was going there on assignment. In a vision, He showed me a road lined with blue diamonds that would take me to His city. He then said I was to prophesy over Sin City with more details to come. The week before our trip, I was spending time in prayer with my eleven-year-old son, who was learning how to use his seer gift. We went on an activation together. We saw ourselves on a red and purple roller coaster descending into hell. Jesus was with us, showing us the strategies of the enemy. My son saw certain demons that were assigned to his life and was able to break his agreement with them and cancel their assignment. Jesus handed me a scroll that I would declare over Satan's den in Las Vegas. Also, the Statue of Liberty appeared, representing the freedom our nation has lost but is being restored. I knew that this restoration had to do with whatever I was going to prophesy when I got to Las Vegas. At the end of the activation, we got off the rollercoaster and climbed up onto the Lion of the tribe of Judah and flew out of hell. The Lord told us that our heart to worship (represented by the lion) would change everything.

Ready for this? Our hotel in Las Vegas was on Blue Diamond Road leading to Zion National Park, just like in the vision I had before we left home. God is amazing! We decided to go into the city to shop and go sightseeing during the day, hoping it would be more kid-friendly. Driving in, we were greeted by the huge lion that sits on the front lawn of the MGM Hotel. Directly across from that stood a Statue of Liberty replica at the New York Hotel, and, of course, next to Lady Liberty was a red and purple roller coaster! You should have seen my son's face when he spotted the rollercoaster. Needless to say, we had to take a ride! That experience made a tremendous impact on my son's young Christian life. We experienced God in an unforgettable way together. By the way, the first thing I realized when I saw the lion and the Statue of Liberty guarding the entrance to Las Vegas is that God is there. He loves that city and its people. Their sin saddens Him, but it doesn't anger or offend him – that's the power of the Cross at work!

Later in the week, my husband surprised me with reservations at The Top of the World restaurant. When I heard the name, I knew immediately that this would be where I would prophesy. The restaurant is situated at the city's highest spot on top of a tower. If you've been there, you're getting an image of what it looks like in your imagination. That's how powerful our imagination is. It will quickly recall our memories as images. We must let God have control of it!

After dinner, we went out to the observation deck to prophesy. I told the others to speak out what was on God's heart for this city.

So we began to speak of God's love, unleashing His heart for Las Vegas from the "top of the world." It was so loud up there, due to the wind, that we couldn't even hear our own voices as we yelled our prophetic words. I noticed amid all the lights and sights that Donald Trump had his name seemingly suspended over it all in big, bold lights: TRUMP. Trump Towers is a tall, gold glass building, which looks like a bar of gold during the day. But at night, the reflection of all the lights on the glass causes the building to blend into the background, leaving only the word TRUMP visible. I chuckled to myself thinking, *what a narcissist!* Immediately, the Lord convicted me saying, "I actually brought you here for this reason." Remember, this was 2008 and a lot has changed for President Donald Trump since then. The Lord told me what I was to declare. So I began,

"Las Vegas, the Lord says, from atop Satan's den, Sin City, He is about to 'TRUMP' the devil at his own game!"

We went back in for dessert and I never really thought about that again until the day Mr. Trump announced he was running for President. When he made his announcement, I thought to myself: *Lord, you couldn't have possibly meant that literally!* But I knew at that moment, that I was looking at the next President of the United States. **God does not think the way we do; He sees things we could never see nor imagine without His revelation. That is what makes Him God and makes serving Him so much fun!** Allowing God to bring you to a place of total surrender is hard, but so worth it. Once you surrender, you see God in amazing ways. Fear blocks all of that from us! In fact, recently, my son was asked in front of a group of people, "What did your parents do to make you want to serve God?" He answered, "While all my other friends said they hated church because it was boring, my parents made serving God fun! God was real to them, and I wanted to have the same kind of joy I saw in them."

If you're not experiencing the fullness of joy God has for you (like my son experienced on our adventures with God), it's time to ask yourself a few questions: "What do I do out of obligation, but I have no real passion or conviction for? Why do I feel compelled to do these things when I really don't want to?"

It's ok if there are Godly things on your list. Healing starts with honesty. God doesn't expect perfection; Jesus covered that. We must be honest, especially with ourselves.

An unsanctified conviction is a conviction that doesn't really come from God.

I describe what we do out of obligation as "unsanctified convictions." Well, I should say Jesus called them that when he started convicting me about mine! An unsanctified conviction comes from our relationship with someone other than God. Our pastors, parents, spouses, schoolteachers, even friends we love and respect, can intentionally or unintentionally take the place of Holy Spirit in our lives. If we are only taught the Word of God through others but we never spend time alone with God ourselves, then our convictions may not be life-giving. Instead, they become energy-demanding. **It takes our own effort to live up to the unsanctified conviction. When Holy Spirit is the one bringing conviction, it is energy producing and life giving. God's grace empowers us to live the conviction.**

So, take that list of obligations you have and start talking to God about those things. Listen for him to show you his heart. If the conviction clearly comes from scripture, then let Holy Spirit reveal your actual thoughts and the healing you may need to receive. If the obligation is a matter of someone else's personal conviction, then ask Holy Spirit how He feels about that conviction for your life.

When God sent Moses into the wilderness with His people, He wanted them all to ascend the mountain. Too afraid, the people insisted that Moses go alone. They preferred for Moses to tell them what to do. They did not pursue their own relationship with God. It is probable that the Father never intended to write the 10 commandments on tablets of stone but on their hearts. "And you show that you are a letter from Christ delivered by us, written not with ink but with the Spirit of the living God, not on tablets of stone but on tablets of human hearts"(2 Corinthians 3:3).

Grace is a power that flows through intimacy with God. He created us for relationship. Apart from that, we are simply religious with no more life than any other religious person. Talk these things out with our heavenly Father who adores you and wants to empower you. He will not be offended by your true thoughts or feelings. He will empower you; simply surrender fear, embrace truth and find joy.

Chapter 8

Embrace the Currency of Heaven: Defeat Hell; Find Joy

I have been a seer and a prophet for many years, long before I understood what I was seeing and how to use this gift in an honorable and edifying way. I have been in the ministry for over thirty years, preaching since I was fourteen. I have made a lot of mistakes, for which I could not be more grateful. Each failure becomes an opportunity to see God and connect with His heart in amazing ways as He refines me in the Refiner's fire.

I am only now willing to surface on a national and international platform because I made a commitment to raise my children and establish their feet firmly in their destinies before I ventured beyond my own personal ministry.

Why do I tell you this? Along the way, I often got tired of waiting; I began to feel left out, dismissed and devalued. Father would have to remind me that He was sticking to the plan and keeping ministry low key for me so I could raise my family. However, being prophetic, I have an intense need for significance. This need set me up for jealousy when other ministers were growing their church and hanging out with "God's Popular Group"! It set me up for abandonment issues. I later discovered that is called an Orphan Spirit.

One vision I had describes being under the Orphan Spirit's influence. Jesus was seated at a beautiful dining table exquisitely decorated with elaborate trimmings and food. At the table were seated various ministry leaders with large well-known ministries. I, however, was dressed as a servant tending to the guests completely unnoticed by all, except Jesus. Jesus would smile and wink at me, trying to make me feel important to him, but instead, it made me furious. At one point, I was in the kitchen prepping for the next course when Jesus came in and gave me a hug, telling me that He appreciated what I was doing for Him, but I shrugged it off. He told me the leaders were being fed by the food I was preparing, which made me very important to Him. I didn't understand then, but I do now. Let me share my journey with you as I share this Word from the Lord to His leaders. May you be fed and nourished by His heart for you.

In another vision, I saw Satan playing the shell game with the church. He was manipulating us and robbing us of our destiny. The Lord said, "The shells are three soulish idols the enemy is using against My church to keep them striving for things they already have and abandoning what they have for things they do not want or need." He called these three soulish idols "The Currency of Hell." These Idols are:

1. **Self-Ambition disguised as Vision**

2. **Self-Preservation disguised as Wisdom**

3. **Self-Condemnation disguised as Humility**

I realize now that the lessons I have learned in obscurity while raising my children, as well as the sin that I needed to repent of, brought me freedom from the currency of hell. Now, I need to deliver this word to God's people.

What Is a Soulish Idol?

Galatians 3:3 (*ESV*) says, "Are you so foolish? Having begun in the Spirit, are you now being made perfect by the flesh?" In other words, we can do good things, even godly things, with soul power, rather than the Spirit. Paul calls this foolish. In Ephesians 3:16, Paul urges us to be strengthened in the inner-man. I have learned that I needed my will to be broken before I could be strengthened in my inner-man or my spirit. Proverbs 3:5,6 tells us not to trust our own understanding but acknowledge God so He can make our path straight. A soulish idol leads us to rely on our self, rather than Holy Spirit, who is to guide us into all truth. So what does this all look like?

For many years, I thought dying to self meant dying to my sin, until Jesus reminded me that He had already done that. Dying to self means letting go of self-effort so that I can be completely controlled by the Spirit of God without getting in His way. This is what the fruit of self-control really is; it is not self-discipline or self-effort. Self-control allows self to be controlled by Holy Spirit. That takes dying daily according to scripture. It is about surrender, not discipline; about receiving, not producing; about exchanging our will for the currency of heaven; rest, remembrance and restoration.

Let's explore how these idols produce a counterfeit work and how the currency of Heaven holds genuine resurrection power. Operating in the currency of heaven will unlock R.E.A.L. Joy.

Self-Ambition Disguised as Vision

Vision: *A Holy Spirit inspired and empowered ability to see God's preferable future. It causes us to obey what God determines is our role and to see that future come to pass.*

The scripture teaches us to seek first the Kingdom of God and then all these things will be added unto us (Matthew 6:33). A genuine vision from Trinity requires us to pursue God and His ways of doing things rather than pursuing our own goals to achieve God's vision.

Self-Ambition: *A strong, self-centered determination to complete an established goal.*

God is both task-oriented and relationship-oriented. We can't impress God with our works like we can with people. God is the one who actually does the work through us or else we have done it without Him, through self-ambition. As a very important side-note, we need to remember that women are created in God's image, too. This means God thinks like a woman, as well. He created us for relationship first. That means Kingdom work should be developing our own intimate relationship with God more than it does for others. Remember, Jesus said, "I no longer call you servant ... but instead I have called you friends" (John 15:15). Like the old saying goes, *it is very easy to get so caught up in the work of God that we forget the God of our work.*

How can I tell the difference?

1. Self-ambition will cause us to finish the vision in the flesh according to worldly standards and for personal gain.

2. Vision is energy-producing; self-ambition is energy-demanding.

Vision hears and obeys, leaving the outcome to God, but self-ambition may hear and obey while also taking responsibility for the outcome. The stress level will cause our hearing to go bad.

Rest Defeats Self-Ambition

The good news is our Father also has a currency originating from Heaven.

In heaven, there is no self-ambition, only rest. God labored for six days and then He rested.

Godly rest is not lack of activity. It is not passivity. It is not laziness or ignorance. Many in the body of Christ think they are at rest, but instead, they are bound in apathy, passivity, and ignorance. In the movie *Lord of the Rings*, the Shire is a good representation of a false rest the church is suffering from. The Hobbits were completely unaware of the battle going on all around them. Frodo was responsible for guarding the ring and taking it back to Mordor, the fires of hell. This would stop the war. The ring is a good example of self-ambition. Frodo met many along the way who wanted to use the power of the ring for good, but the ring always ended up corrupting them instead. Frodo knew that the only way to end the war was to get rid of the ring.

This is our battle, as well. We may want to do good through self-ambition, but that will only corrupt our true identity. Paul says, "We are acting like mere men, because of our petty jealousy and envy" (1 Corinthians 3:3). These sins rob us of the power of the Holy Spirit and generate the idol of self-ambition. Jesus says, "Come unto me all you who labor and are heavy laden and I will give you rest" (Matthew 11:28). There's that word "heavy" or weight again. Remember Hebrews 12, where God instructs us to cast off the weight. He wants us to rest in His glory.

Genuine rest is best explained by the following story I once heard. A Bible translator was struggling to find a word for "believe" in the local dialect he was working with. While in his office, a native friend came into the room and sat down. Then, in the local dialect, he said, "'It feels good to put my full weight into this chair.'" At that point, the Bible translator knew the word for "full weight" was the word he could use for "believe."

To believe in God means we put our full weight in Him.

Now, let's go back to Hebrews 12:1 that instructs us to cast off the weight that entangles us (Hebrews. 12:1). We are to cast off Satan's counterfeit glory in exchange for the weight of God's glory.

We have also talked about the Fruit of the Spirit called "meekness", which means to surrender to the goodness of God. I likened "meekness" to gravity, because the weight of God's glory pulls everything we need towards us. When we carry God's glory, we become weighty in our worth because we have surrendered to the goodness of God. Now, we can see that to believe in God means to put our full weight in Him. *That* is rest!

His glory does all the work, not our self-effort. The biblical idea of rest is to completely believe in God by putting our full weight in His power, without bracing ourselves in case He doesn't come through.

You know you have moved from rest to self-ambition when your adrenaline or anxiety rises because of fear of failure, rejection or stress. It takes surrender to get back to rest so that God can direct our steps instead of a knee- jerk reaction to life!

How do we rest?

There are three lies that will rob us of the joy of the Lord and resting in Him.

1. **I must do everything right.**

2. **Everything must go right.**

3. **Everyone must treat me right.**

By believing these lies, we will produce high levels of self-ambition to stabilize our constantly shifting peace. Aggression, depression, anxiety, fear, and control are all issues generated by these lies. To rest, we must break our agreement with them. In the next chapter, we will focus on how to get free from the lies that steal our joy, preventing genuine rest in our lives.

Self-Preservation Disguised as Wisdom

The second idol of the soul realm is self-preservation, which the enemy disguises as wisdom. Most of us have had our fair share of rejection and betrayal; some have had *more* than a fair share. The old saying goes, "Fool me once; shame on you, fool me twice; shame on me." In an attempt to avoid being fooled or betrayed again, we often establish walls that hinder intimacy with the body of Christ and, more importantly, Trinity. These walls can appear to be wisdom. We may think that we are building safe boundaries, but there is a difference between a wall and a boundary. A wall is a vow we make to protect us, such as *I will never allow someone to hurt me like that again*. A wall causes us to avoid people, situations and opportunities in an attempt to stay safe. A boundary, on the other hand, empowers us to trust people and work with them without fear.

Rejection is a rite of passage; it can bring you into a new level of spiritual authority. Embracing it as something God uses as a tool will allow healing to take place in your heart from the wounds. Not embracing it as from God can lead to witchcraft (manipulation and control). Rejection is meant to expose and protect us from self-ambition, self-condemnation, and self-preservation.

God uses rejection to reveal our weak spots so we become aware and can be healed. The devil uses rejection to reveal other people's weak spots so we can become self-contained, powerless, and at the mercy of those who have hurt us. We must run into God, allowing Him to be our refuge rather than walk in self-preservation.

So, what is self-preservation exactly?

Self-preservation is a state of isolation brought on by rejection, resulting in a strong desire and self-centered determination to maintain one's present condition. Those with that mindset find no delight in understanding, but rather only in expressing one's own heart (see Proverbs 18:1-2). Life often teaches us that it is wise to avoid people, refusing to trust our hearts to anyone. Yet the scripture teaches us differently in 1 John 1:5-7, "God is light and in Him there is no darkness... If we walk in the light as He is in the light we have fellowship with one another and the blood of Jesus cleanses us from all sin."

Based on the NT Greek understanding of this passage we could also say it like this:

"God is truth and in Him there is no deception. If we walk in the truth as He walks in the truth, we have fellowship with one another and the blood of Jesus cleanses us from all sin."

"Deception" is presenting ourselves in the best possible light. In doing so, we will leave certain truth out and manipulate situations and people to avoid that truth from surfacing. We do this on a subconscious level as a result of our pride. We do not want people to know who we really are from fear of rejection. Most of us think our deception helps our relationships, but that is because we do not trust people with the truth.

Deception is presenting ourselves in the best possible light.

Let me give you an example of the deception of self-preservation. When I was a young mother and pastor, I struggled with punctuality. If I was running late to a meeting, I would try to come up with a good enough excuse that would make me look as good as I could in the situation. I told myself I didn't want to make the person feel like they weren't important to me, so I sought to deceive them in order to preserve my relationship with them. It was about that time that the Lord revealed this passage in 1 John, telling me, "People would rather you just state the truth, and so do I."

When I thought about it, I realized I was just trying to protect myself from criticism. True humility is not thinking less of ourselves; it is thinking of ourselves less often. We have all experienced being deceived. We can usually tell when people are lying or keeping something from us. We all long for people to openly admit when they are wrong, and most would probably respect them and forgive them if they did. Yet, when we need to admit wrong, it can feel so degrading that we often resort to deception-thinking like, "Others will not respect us if we tell the truth." We must abandon self-preservation, which comes from fear of rejection generated by our pride. We must yield to the truth of God's Word. Walk in truth rather than deception. Do not masquerade with an excuse or cast blame when wrong. Instead, repent and present a solution. This is respectful and will, in most cases, earn respect from others. Life becomes easier when we are not managing our walls and going to war with people who see past them. Let go of self-preservation and get joy and rest in God, your defender!

What is genuine wisdom?

Wisdom can be defined as the soundness of an action or decision with regard to the application of experience and knowledge. According to Proverbs 1:7, wisdom begins with the Spirit of the fear of the Lord. In Isaiah 11, the Spirit of the fear of the Lord is one of the seven Spirits of Holy Spirit. The Spirit of the fear of the Lord empowers us to recognize sinful thoughts, feelings and beliefs that are grounded in worldly wisdom. They may appear sound because of hurtful experiences, but they are not biblical. Walking with Holy Spirit will teach us to repent rather than make excuses for our actions. We tend to have more of a desire to be changed by people and situations rather than to change our situation and the people we think are the problem.

Many years ago, I was facing persecution from the denomination I was a part of at the time. They were godly people, but they were unaccepting of prophetic ministry or anyone who accepted the call to such an office. It was very difficult to keep my heart free from offense because no one confronted me personally, but they were quite vocal from their pulpits. I could have felt justified in using my pulpit to retaliate. But the Spirit of the fear of the Lord led me to honor them publicly and privately. This often felt humiliating, but I am so thankful for all that I learned. That experience helped me mature spiritually and gain authority in my calling. **It is time for the church to walk with the Spirit of the fear of the Lord so that we honor God more than our own interests.** God will protect us when we stop trying to do it ourselves! Self-Preservation is often disguised as wisdom. We must invite the spirit of the fear of the Lord to bring conviction and illuminate the difference for us.

Rejoicing defeats self-preservation

In addition to rest, the currency of Heaven includes rejoicing! The Hebrew mindset is one of celebration for all that God has done. Our western culture, influenced by a Greek mindset, centers on production. When we have been hurt, we tend to isolate and pull back from being productive. Our Greek culture demands us to pull ourselves up by the bootstraps and get moving. As result, the guilt can keep us trapped. Look at the role that rejoicing plays in walking intimately with Father. The Psalmist tells us to enter His courts with thanksgiving and His gates with praise (Psalm 100:4). Also, Jesus shows us in The Lord's Prayer to start with rejoicing and thanksgiving for who God is (Matthew 6:9). Rather than being walled in by self-preservation, we need to let a joyful heart arise by focusing on the blessings and benefits of our walk with God.

Holy Spirit is our comforter and He loves to make us rejoice. He fills my heart with delight at the lengths he will go to lift my spirit. Holy Spirit will let us know how valuable we are to Him. It makes us rejoice.

Let me share one such experience I have had walking with the Comforter. Perry and I were on vacation in San Francisco. We took a self-guided tour to Alcatraz, listening on a headset device to the voice of a former actual prisoner guide us through the abandoned prison. We got to a large window that overlooked the city

> *Holy Spirit loves to make us rejoice. He goes to great lengths to show us our value to Him.*

across the bay. The voice said solemnly, "This was the loneliest place in the prison because from here you could see the sights and hear the sounds of the city, but you couldn't get to it." I started to cry an ugly, uncontrollable cry. That's how *I* felt at the time. I could see the sights and sounds of God's holy city but I couldn't get to it. I wanted heaven to come to earth. I wanted revival for our nation but just couldn't get to it.

The next day we were driving around and found ourselves at the corner of Haight and Ashbury. If you're a hippie at heart, you know exactly where we were. The Summer of Love started on that street corner, back in the 60s. At the time, over 100,000 teenagers descended on the little park for apparently no reason. It birthed the sexual revolution and the hippie scene. That summer changed our nation and set us on an ungodly path from which we have yet to recover.

Standing there, I asked Holy Spirit, "What was here that drew all those kids?" He said, "It wasn't what was here, it was what was not here." He continued, "There was no religious spirit in this town." Trinity wanted to breathe fresh air on that generation which would have birthed the summer of unconditional love, but the church reacted in fear; the religious people reacted. They tried to use fear to keep the kids from being deceived, and it pushed them right into it. Instead, it ended up being the summer of unconditional sex.

The Lord told me that He brought us there on assignment to prophesy to the land. I declared in the place where the nation got off track that it would be put back on it! Revival was coming to San Francisco. I asked the Lord why me since I have no connection to this city. I am from Ohio. He said, "Yes, but your city is a stop on Interstate 80. It starts at the Golden Gate Bridge and ends in New York." **I knew He was telling me the revival would spread across the country along Interstate 80 and we would be a part of it.** I was rejoicing by faith, but when I got back to Ohio, things became more clear.

Perry and I decided to go see the movie *The Book of Eli* when we got home. The movie starts thirty years after the earth has been nearly destroyed by a nuclear war. Few have survived who can remember what the world was like before. With the world full of savages, books are the only connection to the once civilized world. One survivor, Eli, has been given the task of guarding a very special, sought after book. Through most of the movie, we do not know what the book is, but its value is attested by fight after brutal fight between people trying to take ownership of this one book that can restore them. Even if you haven't seen the movie, you probably have guessed by now that the book was the Bible!

Why am I telling you this? Well, during the entire movie, Eli is traveling on a broken, washed-out road. He is taking the Bible to an unknown destination for an unknown reason, but he just knows he has to go. He picks up a traveling companion and teaches her the Word. He tells her repeatedly that we walk by faith and not by sight.

As I watched the movie, God was beginning to speak to me again, comforting me. My heart was rejoicing! As the movie draws to an end, Eli is wounded and the book is stolen. It is then that we learn Eli's book is written in braille because he is blind. He really did walk by faith and not by sight.

God had protected His Word from getting into the wrong hands, by making the only surviving copy written in braille. Eli, now dying, struggles to continue his journey, but he is undisturbed by the fact that the Book was stolen. This becomes significant at the end. As they continue to travel on this broken highway, the scenery is getting familiar. I turned to Perry and said, "If this is Napa Valley and the road he's been traveling is Route 80, I am gonna flip!" Sure enough

... he comes out on to the Golden Gate Bridge and takes the Bible to Alcatraz!

At Alcatraz, a group of people have reassembled an old-fashioned printing press. The movie ends with the first printed copy of the Bible being placed on a shelf marked "Alcatraz Press." Eli dies, but not before he quoted the entire Bible, having memorized it by heart. I was crying with delight. As Eli's friend takes a copy of the Bible, armed with the Word, she heads out to change the world!

What great lengths God had gone to comfort me! It felt like He made a whole movie for me! **He told me, "From Alcatraz, from the place of your brokenness, the revival will come!"** Even now, as I pen these words, I am overwhelmed at the magnitude of God's love! I am rejoicing as He sings over us with songs of deliverance. Let God rejoice over you! He will comfort you, protect you, and fill you with joy so you won't have to struggle with self-preservation!

Self-Condemnation Disguised as Humility

The third idol of the soul realm is self-condemnation, which means "to express complete disapproval of, to declare someone unfit for use, to sentence to a particular punishment." Self-condemnation made me feel like I needed to sit down, shut up, and wear beige. The Lord began to show me how I kept exchanging the anointing for humility. Every time a prideful thought came to my mind, I would stop letting the Lord use me by telling myself I was too prideful to be effective for God. It was easy for the devil to stop me from being who God wanted me to be. All he had to do was convince me I was prideful of using my gifts. We have to learn to rebuke pride but not disqualify ourselves from walking in the anointing God has chosen to place on our life.

How do we recognize self-condemnation?

We can often think self-condemnation is conviction from God. Self-condemnation is an evil master requiring us to walk with inferiority. That does not come from our Father in Heaven who empowers us with powerful gifts (Romans 12). We are designed to use these gifts as we mature in our faith, not after we've matured. Romans 12 reveals seven

Let God rejoice over you. He will comfort you, protect you, fill you with joy... so you won't have to struggle!

DNA gifts given by Father. He requires us to use them according to our level of faith. I have a DNA gift mix of Prophet and Servant. For many years I struggled with an internal battle between the very different perspectives in these two gifts. I can best describe this turmoil with a vision I had that reveals my personal struggle with self-condemnation.

In the vision, I saw my prophetic gift as a very intimidating bee-keeper. I was powerful and scary looking, with tattoos and large muscles. Bees were swarming a young woman, and I was fearlessly hosing her off with a fire hose. She was screaming for me to stop because the water was stinging her more than the bees. I ignored her because I knew the water wouldn't kill her, but the bees might! At the same time, I saw my servant gift as a refined version of myself sitting behind a desk. My servant gift was speaking very gently to the woman, as to not offend her, but was having no effect on her or the bees. Yet the servant part of me felt good about the fact that I was able to remain calm in the situation, demonstrating gentleness and patience. Once the prophetic version of myself, represented by the beekeeper, freed the woman from the bees, the woman was very grateful. However, my servant gift, represented by the refined version of myself, was disgusted by the beekeeper's behavior and sat very smugly, speaking with condemnation to both the beekeeper and the girl who needed to be rescued. My servant side felt ignored by both the prophet and the girl being attacked.

I realize now that Holy Spirit brought healing and maturity to both my prophetic gift and servant gift through that tug of war on the inside. As iron sharpens iron, the two different perspectives inside of me sharpened each other. Now, I am both a prophet with a softer approach and a servant that isn't afraid to be bold. The Holy Spirit has given me a new image of myself that suits how he sees me. To Trinity I am like a red cardinal in a tree. The red cardinal, with his bold color, causes the predator to be distracted, and run after him instead of those he is protecting. I serve others by protecting them with my prophetic gift. So, what internal conversation is going on inside of you? Are you being refined in the fire or oppressed by your imperfections?

Walk in True Humility

> You study the Scriptures diligently because you think that in them you have eternal life. These are the Scriptures that testify about me (Jesus), yet you refuse to come to me to have life ... But do not think I will accuse you before the Father. Your accuser is Moses (referring to the law), on whom your hopes are set. –John 5:39-40,45 (NIV)

Self-condemnation is generated by the letter of the law, whereas Jesus is the Spirit of the Law. As the above scripture points out, diligently studying the Word should lead us to depend on Jesus. However, if it leads you to feeling disapproved of, that condemnation does not come from Jesus. It comes from a religious view that sees the Word as laws one must keep rather than a Person to trust in. True humility comes from confidence and safety in the love of Jesus. It frees us to be known for who we really are, nothing more and nothing less. Arrogance and insecurity are just different expressions of a prideful heart. If you walk

So what internal conversation is going on inside of you? Are you being refined in the fire or oppressed by your imperfections?

in arrogance, you will think more highly of yourself, making excuses for failure, rendering Holy Spirit unable to move you. If you walk in insecurity, you will think less of yourself, exempting yourself to avoid failure, rendering Holy Spirit unable to move you. When you embrace your God-given identity and gifting, you will honor God in success and accept failure. Genuine humility keeps you learning and allowing Holy Spirit to move you. Once you shed self-condemnation, it will become easier to be yourself and trust Jesus to make up the difference.

Remembrance Defeats Self-Condemnation

What you remember, you will reproduce. We must remember the cross, His unfailing love and grace when we feel defeated. The enemy can so easily use our imagination to lead us into fear with "what ifs," "oh nos," and "how comes." When fear dominates our imagination, we easily lose sight of all that God has done. We must choose to give God access to our imagination by remembering what He has done and has said in His Word. **We must not lose in the darkness what God shows us in the light.** We must take every thought captive to the obedience of Christ. We can do this by opening our imagination and allowing God to speak with images. When we receive a picture of the Word of God, it makes a lasting impression. It can be recalled much easier than a concept. This is why Jesus spoke with parables. He was accessing the listeners' imagination and leaving a memorable image. All good preachers use illustrations and stories. When you are alone with God, let Him speak to you in picture form as it will help you remember His truths.

For example, in worship I saw an image in my mind's eye of myself holding the world on my shoulders. The Lord said, "You cannot carry your anointing." Immediately I saw the world change into a sleigh beneath my feet. Father then spoke, "Let your anointing carry you!" This is what I remember when I am feeling overwhelmed by ministry. I cannot shoulder it. I must let God's anointing carry me through. Give God, instead of the devil, access to your imagination. Remember God and defeat self-condemnation!

I bless you to walk in genuine vision, wisdom and humility — the currency of heaven. Heaven's currency produces rest in God, joyful remembrance for all that God is and does, and empowers us with res-urrection power. May you encounter the Spirit of the Fear of the Lord who will expose the currency of Hell and free you from the soulish Idols of Self-Ambition, Self-Preservation and Self-Condemnation, which align you with the enemy, who comes to steal joy. As I see the tide rising and the winds of change stirring, heaven is unleashing a current of the Father's thoughts intended to sweep His Bride up into the arms of her savior. May you have ears to hear and eyes to see what Father is saying in this hour. May your spirit be nourished with these words and your soul aligned with the currency of heaven. Be released from the turbulence of the soul realm, resting in your identity as a Son of God and the Bride of Christ. Get joy through the currency of heaven.

Chapter 9

Embrace Your Own Heart: Discover the Three Lies that Steal Joy

"He is everywhere while He is nowhere, for 'Where' has to do with matter and space and God is independent of both. He is unaffected by time or motion, is wholly self-dependent and owes nothing to the worlds His hands have made" (A.W. Tozer).

I love the way Tozer writes. He captures the majesty and awe of Trinity. If you allow yourself to ponder God as Mary did, glory moves about, aligning your body and mind to His message. He is everywhere but not as an indifferent observer or an uptight mastermind. God knows all and can control all, but He doesn't have to control anything. He is supportive, comforting, wise, and completely hands-off at the same time. It all depends on our observation, not His!

How do you observe God? How you see Him changes everything. We can rise no higher than our concept of God. Fearing change or failure, along with a constant need to be right, stems from a small view of God. See God as He is, and you see everything as it should be, most of all, how you see yourself. God is delighted with you. He's not angry or disappointed. He knows you and all your ways better

> *If you allow yourself to ponder God like Mary did, glory moves about, and your body and mind align with His message.*

than you do. The fact that you are continuing to journey deep into this book tells me you are after intimacy with Trinity and your passion to know God supersedes your religious notions and fear of man. I know the things in this book will not be accepted by everyone. You probably don't accept everything I have said, either. That's good! I could be wrong! That's the whole point of walking with God! Faith takes risk and complete trust that God is our redeemer. Trinity is delighted with people who are passionate to know Him; the cross covers their failures along the way. Jesus took issue with the Pharisees, the ones who thought they knew God and were completely confident they had their theology straight. The Pharisees were passionate about being right and appearing righteous even if they missed the savior they were hoping for in the process. However, you are a seeker of the true God or you wouldn't have come this far in this journey with me. Thanks for hearing me out. My prayer is that I inspire you to go after the deep things of the Spirit. I am totally Ok if you can't embrace everything being said here.

We don't have to agree with each other, but we must love each other. The rich inheritance we have in the saints is essential to our walk with God. Paul penned a large portion of the New Testament, developing most of our theology of right and wrong. In his prayers for us, he prays for revelation so we can experience the rich inheritance we have in the saints through the power that raised Jesus from the dead.

> I keep asking that the God of our Lord Jesus Christ, the glorious Father, may give you the Spirit of wisdom and revelation, so that you may

know him better. I pray that the eyes of your heart may be enlight-ened in order that you may know the hope to which he has called you, the riches of his glorious inheritance in his holy people, and his incomparably great power for us who believe. That power is the same as the mighty strength he exerted when he raised Christ from the dead and seated him at his right hand in the heavenly realms. – Ephesians 1:17-20 (*NIV*)

We could be enjoying our relationships so much more if it weren't for the three lies that steal our joy and hinder us from walking in the Spirit of revelation and wisdom that Paul desired for us. I mentioned these lies in the previous chapter, but let's take a closer look.

Three Lies that Steal Our Joy

1. "I must do everything well."

2. "Everything must go well."

3. "Everyone must treat me well."

Lie 1: "I must do everything well."

Live by this lie and life will be riddled with anxiety, blame, fear of failure, deception, and a host of toxic perspectives. It takes all these things to maintain this horrible illusion that it is possible to do everything well! The saddest thing about believing this lie is how much love and joy you will miss out on because there is simply too much at stake to risk failure.

I hear people who believe this lie say all the time, "Oh, I'm just hard on myself but not others." That, my friend, is a part of this lie. Jesus says, "Love others as you love yourself" (Matthew 22:39). We can-not give to others what we do not give ourselves. If you're hard on yourself, you will be disappointed and offended by the failures of others. Failure on someone else's part will feel like rejection on your part. We will imagine that people just didn't care enough to do the right thing. Loving people fail. Good people fail. You fail!

If we want to be a safe place for others, we need to be one for ourselves first. I was involved with street ministry at the beginning of my career. I spent time in the red light district of several nations preaching the gospel in bars and brothels. I loved it, but as I matured in my relationship with God, I realized that my calling to the streets did more for me than for God or anyone else. That was a problem I needed to be courageous enough to look at. I wanted to make excuses and I did for a while, but God always wins those battles in the end, right?

So, I let God reveal my heart. I prayed as David did, "Search my heart, oh God, and see if there be any wicked way in me" (Psalms 139:23-24). He revealed that I had no grace for the church. I liked being with "pre-Christians" as we say today. They were easy to love. I expected them to sin, fail, be angry, etc. but I expected the saints to be better than that. Sure, we need grace, but at some point, one should move beyond that, right? Well, I knew I needed grace still, but I carried so much guilt and shame over my sin. I wore the guilt like a badge of honor. I told myself that at least I cared when I failed. To me, most everyone else in the church didn't seem to care at all about their sin! WOW! What a load of *#@&*! Please don't be offended by my explicit communication. In a vision, I literally saw a huge dung heap full of maggots and horrible things. It smelled horrible, too, as you could imagine. That was one time I wished the gift of discerning of spirits did not include actually smelling something in the spirit realm. I asked Holy Spirit, "What is that?" He said, "Your spiritual pride." God showed me my thought process stunk like dung!

Jesus told me, "You would return to your sin like a dog to its vomit if it weren't for My grace. You will never outgrow the need for that grace, so cut the guilt trip. It's not helping, and it sure isn't humility." Our guilt stems from the fact that we actually think we can be better than human. That's spiritual pride! We don't have that potential; that's why we need a savior. When we accept that, we can move on.

I learned from that experience that the devil is the one that wants us to feel guilty. God just wants us to accept that we are. Here is a good indication that you're struggling with the lie that you have to do everything well. Ask yourself, "What would I do if I overheard someone speaking to my child the way I speak to myself?" Not only must we

Our guilt stems from the fact that we actually think we can be better than human. That's spiritual pride!

accept that we fail; we need to learn to be kind to ourselves when we do. Kindness doesn't make excuses. Kindness helps us fall forward, learn from our mistakes, and continue in our destiny.

This lie of "A Spirit of Excellence" keeps us from reaching our full potential because we learn to identify ourselves by our failures as we strive for excellence. That's why I hate this "spirit of excellence" slogan. Most often I have seen it directed at "motivating" (judging) someone else, not even ourselves! Excellence has nothing to do with having to do everything the right way. **Excellence is about honor, grace, love — the things that make the Kingdom of God great! If I lose honor or respect for myself or others because of failure, I sure am not acting in the excellence of God!** We would be toast if that were to happen! We fail, others fail; but success is staying engaged in the process. We all have the desire to do well, but the key is how do I feel when it goes wrong? In that moment, can I admit it and fix it or do I hide behind excuses because I can't face the failure? How long does it take to get back up on the horse?

If you want a good book to read about breaking the power of this lie, I would suggest *Daring Greatly* by Dr. Brene Brown. Dr. Brown has done comprehensive research on the effect of shame brought on by this lie and others. I warn you it will be the toughest book you'll ever love if you have the courage to face your failures. Remember that Paul the Apostle said he had learned to boast in his weaknesses (2 Corinthians 12:9). He had learned the joy of discovering the power of God and His love because of his own flaws and failures. R.E.A.L. joy comes when I can face failure, recover quickly, and move forward.

Lie 2: "Everything must go well."

Jesus says, "Peace I leave with you; My peace I give unto you, not as the world gives, give I unto you. Let not your heart be troubled, neither let it be afraid" (John 14:27). The peace Jesus gives is different than the peace the world gives...hmmm. Like happiness, worldly peace is temporal, based on our situation rather than our relationship with Jesus. As we mentioned earlier, joy is found not from pursuing *it*, but rather pursuing God. Peace works the same way. We all know that if we pursue patience, all hell breaks loose, and we are anything but patient!

Peace can only be found by pursuing God's heart. If I believe that everything needs to go well, which usually means *my way*, then I will seek peace through controlling my situation instead of allowing God to control it.

Jesus leaves His peace with us. That means He has already given it to me, but my incessant need to control my circumstances will always steal my peace. God and I cannot be in control at the same time. Fear causes my need for control. It is a knee-jerk reaction that steals the peace of God from us. This causes us to hinder what God is trying to do in our situation. We must surrender fear to have peace and joy.

Jesus urges us to not let our hearts be troubled or afraid. It's a choice. Anxiety should not control us. We should be controlling our anxiety. We all get stressed, and stress produces anxiety, but I do not have to be controlled by it! Demanding and expecting that things always go your way will create an extremely stressful burden. This

> *Jesus leaves His peace with us. We already have it. But our need to control the outcome steals our peace.*

burden will have us trying to put out all the fires we think are threatening our peace, but the problem is that they keep popping up. You manage to put one fire out and the next one comes soon after. I hear people say all the time, "I would be happy if only…" This is not the kind of peace that comes from Jesus. He never promised life would go our way. In fact, He promised tribulation, persecution, and carrying our cross. Clearly, when Jesus promised peace, He did not mean everything would go well!

When my daughter was 14, she started to become angry, avoiding the family, and hiding in her room. She was mainly mad at God because she has always had a big heart for people and was struggling with their unresolved pain. However, her anger became directed towards me. I couldn't do anything well in her eyes. One day she told me, "I don't need you in my life, so leave me alone."

I know God was with me because I stayed calm, even though it shot like a knife through my heart. I said, "Ok, if that is how you feel, let's come up with an arrangement. If you don't want me as your mom, you can live here as our boarder. I know you can't afford rent so you can work for me around the house to cover it, but we will have to increase your chores. Also, there are several things I tolerate as your mother, but I wouldn't as your landlord. For example, no loud music in your room, no free cell phone, and no free rides around town. I do not need to chauffeur a boarder, but you can come and go as you please." Needless to say, that arrangement didn't last long. The next day she told me that I had misunderstood what she meant. Watching your adolescent begin to test out their independence can provide some hilarious memories.

Seriously, that was a very painful 24 hours; I remember crying myself to sleep. I didn't know what she would do next, but I knew I could not control her in order to find peace. I could have screamed and yelled, which I have done as well. I could have poured the guilt on like the old country song, "For the nine months I carried you, no charge." The reality is, when we seek to control our situation (and people), we usually serve to stir up strife instead of peace. I learned with Carley that trying to control her behavior only made her want to rebel more, as with most people. I learned a great deal about myself, raising kids. I had to learn to break my agreement with the lie that things had to go well or my way. Seeking God for His peace brings about His plan! For more on raising kids God's way, check out Danny Silk's book, *Loving Your Kids on Purpose.*

I wish I could say things got better right away with Carley, but they didn't. She began cutting herself as a means of dealing with her anger. I will never forget the day I discovered the terrifying sight on her thighs. Several of the cuts should have had stitches. You may be thinking, *Well, if you had done something about her issues earlier, that wouldn't have happened!* That is usually the fear that takes over. We think that if we don't *do something*, it will get worse. Pain is an amazing tutor if we are not afraid of it. Carley and I learned more about God, ourselves and our destinies through her situation. Even now as I share our story, the emotion is deep, but it's not painful anymore. I am thankful to Jesus, who taught me how to release my control in a season of my life when I wanted to hang on for dear life!

The tears are flowing as I scribe this, but with great joy. Jesus rescued my daughter in a most profound and beautiful way — more about that later! Now, she is on the global staff of our ministry and a phenomenal worship leader. She has a heart for missions as she has begun to travel the world sharing Jesus. I am amazed by the beautiful woman of God that she has become.

I am most grateful for the opportunity that terrible situation gave God to become more to me and my family than I had ever experienced before. R.E.A.L. Joy comes when we respond entirely to the affections of the Lord, instead of to our fear and need to have things go our way.

I know it would not have turned out this way if I had demanded things to "go well!" When Carley was battling, Holy Spirit told me not to take scissors or demonic music away from her. What?! There was no way allowing her to keep these things would bring me peace in my mind. I would pray and cry and pray, and repeat. I didn't even feel like she was safe in our own home. **The Lord told me He would produce a heart of worship in her through her pain if I listened to Him.** However, if I insisted on trying to protect her my way by taking away music, those unsaved friends, etc., she was more likely to hate me and God! I also knew that if I followed conventional wisdom by having her put on medication and letting the psychologists label her with some disorder, she would struggle the rest of her life. **In spite of all the challenges, deep down inside, I had peace; I was confident God's ways were better than mine. It was so hard to give God control and let go of having things my way.** This is what it means in Philippians 4:7 when it says His peace surpasses all understanding. Often, we just have to trust what God is telling us to do, even when it doesn't make sense to our finite minds.

Let me stop here to say that if you have a child struggling with this addiction, **don't just do what I did,** thinking that if it worked in our situation, it will work in yours. Don't do what you think you should do or what anyone else tells you to do. Listen to God, and do what He says to do. What worked for my child may not be what will work for your child. Only God knows; let go of the control and go to God. If you're not secure in your ability to hear God, then go to someone who does. Ask them to help you discern God's voice.

> *If you're insecure in your ability to hear God's voice, go to someone who does and ask them to help you discern God's voice.*

Because I heard God and was obedient to Him, I received His comfort and His peace. He was always reassuring me that He was working all of this together for Carley's good. I knew, as painful and scary as it was, that it was all a part of her journey that would equip her to fulfill her destiny. God was going to teach her and prepare her through all of this. I had His peace; I couldn't let the devil steal it! The fear was intense at times, and I made mistakes along the way, but I wouldn't change that time in my life for anything.

Carley now ministers to young women who struggle with cutting. She has even seen the scars of those she prays for disappear right before her eyes! Personally, she loves her scars; they are a reminder of Jesus her savior and how He saved her.

Lie 3: "Everyone must treat me well."

Of course, most of us would never admit we battle with this one! But the truth is that our expectations will never be met in this regard. Just look at how often you fail to treat others well... ouch! We fail, even with the best intentions at times. The culture we live in is raising a generation of highly offendable people. We keep trying to protect ourselves from offense with political correctness. Wow, is everyone offended these days. Look, I am a Christian, so I don't worship Buddha, but if I go into a Chinese restaurant, I can't ask the owner to remove His Buddha! If I don't want to be around a Buddha, I can choose another restaurant.

If you want to protect your child from abusive behavior, teach them to respect themselves enough to recognize abusive people and stay away. Teach them how to forgive when they feel offended. Teach them that they do not have to accept the negative opinions of others. We cannot seek to control every single person, so that we are never mistreated. All we are doing is becoming easily offended; it's making us weaker as a nation; not kinder. I find many politically correct advocates to be extremely rude and disrespectful in their attempt to defend and protect people from rudeness and disrespect. We must break free from the lie that "everyone needs to treat me well"!

Here's the truth: in this life you will be hurt by others. We cannot help being hurt when someone does or says something hurtful. **Some people have been trained to think that if you admit you're hurt, then you are weak. This is a lie that ends up creating a lot of**

internal anger and rejection. This state of mind sets a person up for an Orphan Spirit. If you need additional help on these subjects, go to **unleashedhealingcenter.com** or **AbbaFather'sLove.com.** For the sake of this book on joy, I will just say that the Orphan Spirit causes a person to detach from relationships they really want to develop, because they can't afford to risk being hurt. We were created for relationship, so when emotional isolation is the weapon used to protect ourselves from rejection, we live in a state of rejection by our own creation.

> *A person in agreement with the Orphan spirit will interpet help from others as disagreement and rejection.*

A person in agreement with the Orphan spirit will interpret feedback and counsel from others as criticism and disagreement; in other words, rejection. No matter what people are doing to develop relationship with this person, it will only serve to create more isolation in their life. For instance, let's say I am trying to help a friend make a decision about her career. I know my friend struggles with anxiety when there are many people around, so if she asks me what I think of her training to become an emergency nurse, I might tell her I don't think that's a good choice for her. I may encourage her to think how she may feel more successful working in a doctor's office, if becoming a nurse is on her heart. A person with an Orphan Spirit would more than likely take offense to that suggestion. She may feel criticized, believing I don't think she would make a good emergency nurse. If I attempt to explain my desire to help her, she may just get more offended at my disagreement with her interpretation of my comment.

This is the kind of people we are developing in our culture. In fact, the enemy is breaking down communications as a standard war strategy to defeat the church! Many are unable to receive help from others and set unrealistic standards regarding how they should be treated by others. The result is a lack of covenant relationships that can build safety, harmony and support in our difficult lives.

> Faithful are the wounds of a friend; but the kisses of an enemy are deceitful. – Proverbs 27:6 (*NKJV*)

This passage states that kisses from an enemy are deceitful. When someone acts nicely towards you, but their intention is to manipulate you, that is the kiss of an enemy.

The politically correct culture is creating deceit by making people nice rather than kind. The word "nice" means agreeable, satisfactory, scrupulous (concerned with doing wrong or appearing wrong to others). A nice person agrees with everyone because they don't want others to think poorly of them. Their real goal is to meet the expectations of others. This is what our ungodly culture wants — agreeable people who won't get in the way. They don't want to appear like a "hater" — the buzzword used in today's culture to describe anyone whose views and convictions don't conform to expectations. Such deception!

Now, let's do a quick biblical word study for "kind" using *Strong's Concordance*.

"Checed" (Hebrew OT): goodness, faithfulness, lovingkindness, mercy.
Goodness: a benefit to others.
Faithfulness: firmness, steadfastness, loyalty
Lovingkindness: considerate of someone's feelings, showing empathy, not easily provoked, showing a readiness to give to others.

Mercy: Giving relief in suffering, to forgive those you have the power to punish.

"Chrēstos" (Greek NT): gentleness, goodness, with ease, not rigid, free from worry or concern.

So, let's put these definitions together to formulate a biblical understanding of "kind." A kind person is a benefit to others, ready to help, firm and steadfast but not easily provoked. A kind person can empathize with others and forgive them. A kind person is at ease and not rigid when dealing with confrontation; they are free from worry or concern that they will not be liked. A kind person can and will disagree when, ultimately, it is beneficial to others' wellbeing. A kind person is loyal enough to speak the truth in love, even if the friend is made to feel uncomfortable. A true friend is faithful to actually help; not merely agree so that they will be liked. This is what we are called to develop in our lives — the fruit of the spirit called "Kindness." This is why the scripture teaches us that the wounds of a friend are faithful.

If you want to experience R.E.A.L. Joy, find a real friend who will be kind, not just nice. R.E.A.L. Joy comes when we allow others to speak the truth in love to us without getting offended. If we want R.E.A.L. Joy in our lives, we must break free from the lie that "everyone needs to treat me well."

If we want R.E.A.L. Joy, it starts with learning to Respond Entirely to the Affections of the Lord. When I am R.E.A.L. with God, I will be R.E.A.L. with myself and break free from the three lies that steal my joy.

Let's Get R.E.A.L. with Others:
Unity Accelerates Joy

Chapter 10

Discover You: Return to Eden; Impart Joy

It was God's good pleasure to create man in His image.

– Genesis 1:26:27

God created man in the Garden of Eden. "Eden" means pleasure of God. Man was made in the pleasure of God's Garden. He delights to fill our lives with His dreams and His purposes; forming our identity, activating our gifts, and releasing our destiny.

God is eternal, which means He has been and always will be without beginning or end. So when God created, He simply activated His eternal dream. We are eternal beings with no beginning or end — a dream released from the heart of God. Each of us has the same opportunity to develop God's dream by being placed temporarily into time, which does have a beginning and end. However, in John 17:16, Jesus states that we are not of this world anymore than He is. Our life on earth is a brief expression of our eternal existence with God. We are small-minded when this temporal life means more to us than our eternal one. Each of us are on the same journey to return to Eden, the place of God's good pleasure, to discover our true identity and destiny.

One day I was taken in the Spirit to a glass room filled with a beautiful substance that is hard to describe. It was pearl-like, cloud-like, and diamond-like, all at the same time. This substance was swirling the room gracefully when I saw the door open, and a human form walked in and stood in the middle of the room. This person had no facial features nor details to their body at all. I watched as this person became enveloped in the swirling substance in the room. The floor opened, and the person fell into space through a portal of some kind. I asked Jesus who was standing with me and He said it was "Conception." The substance was the person's DNA, which was coded with everything they had agreed to become during their temporal stay on earth. Conception is for sure a glorious, intentional, highly personal experience in which no human has a right to intervene.

God uses our highly limited imagination, so when we experience visions, we are seeing things that can only be described with our human experience. For example, when John says in Revelation that he saw a huge locust with an iron breast,[8] He didn't know what a helicopter was because it hadn't been invented yet, so he described what he saw with his limited imagination. So, my description of conception is also limited. However, it can be a great visual for helping us understand how our identity and destiny are intertwined, making us fearfully and wonderfully made (Psalm 139:14).

In the Garden of Eden, man was created in the image of God. This means several things, but for our purposes here, we are looking at the word "image," which means a mental or actual picture of someone/something formed, either physically through sculpture,

---

8 Revelation 9:9

painting, or photography or formed in the mind. Therefore, Trinity had an image in Their mind and formed man from clay based on the vision of Their mind. We are a part of God's imagination. God fashioned a physical replica of who He is and that is us. God is spirit, meaning He had no physical form until He fashioned man in His image.

> *Go back to Eden, the garden of God's pleasure, and recover your true identity. Take your position in Christ.*

We are not our own. We have identity in God and a destiny to fulfill. **It is pure selfishness to live detached from the true identity and destiny that our DNA has encoded within us. We have a responsibility to go back to the future.** We must connect with Trinity and allow Holy Spirit to reveal our eternal identity and destiny to us so that we can fulfill it.

Our identity and destiny are within us. Discovery of these starts with acknowledging our truest passions and longings. They can be found in the lost dreams of our childhood before life corrupted our hope. I am not suggesting that we're all supposed to be ballerinas and superheroes, so don't go dig out your old tutu and red cape. I am saying to let your heart dream again. Life has a tendency to drain us of our childlike faith. We exchange dreams for responsibilities and call it growing up, yet back in our childhood dreams, the sparks of destiny and identity existed. Let Holy Spirit take you back to your future. He will rekindle the life that has been lost and restore the joy that comes from walking in our true identity and destiny.

True Identity

God created a clay model or image of Himself in you. **You have received a specific part of who God really is and when you identify**

it, activate and release it, that part of God is made known in the earth. Misty Edwards wrote a song called "Favorite One." The lyrics best describe this partnership we have with God. "Jesus, Here I am, your favorite one, What are You thinking, what are You feeling? I have to know." Meditating on that song, I asked Jesus how everyone could be His favorite one. He simply said, "You were each given a specific part of Trinity that no one else has, so when I fellowship with you, we become one. When you release the part of Me I gave you, that makes you My favorite." The same can be true for everyone.

Unfortunately, most of us struggle between our position in Christ and our experience in life. Ephesians 2:6 says we are seated with Christ in heavenly places. Romans 8:36 calls us more than conquerors. Romans 6:14 says, "Sin no longer has dominion over [us]." These are just a few scriptures that speak of our position in Christ. Life, on the other hand, has spoken many things over us that can steal the truth of our position, causing us to wander through life. We have the ability to choose what we set our mind on. Colossians 3:2 instructs us to set our mind on things above (position) not on things below (experience). Philippians 4:8 states that we are to only think about the things that are pure, lovely and of good report. And let's not make the same huge mistake the Israelites made and believe the 10 fearful spies instead of God Himself! (See Numbers 13-14.) Yet, how often do we allow our imagination to be set on the bad report? How often do we disregard the kind and encouraging words of a friend who sees our potential because we think to ourselves, "They don't know the real me"? Actually, we are the ones blinded by life. It's time to believe the good reports and ignore the bad ones.

If you want to walk in your true identity, it goes back to "denying self." Jesus said we must deny ourselves in order to follow Him. We must stop believing the negative, powerless things we have been trained to think about ourselves. Deny that stuff and follow what Jesus says instead. It's time to deny our experiences in life that have only served to blind us regarding our position in Christ. We cannot fight *for* our position; we must fight *from* it. There is no power in our temporal experience; the power is in our eternal position. We have it, so believe in it no matter what experience has said.

My experiences in life taught me to sit down, shut up and wear beige, meaning to just blend in and not cause waves. I am a prophetic woman in a largely old-school religious, ethnic city. In the natural, the mafia ruled for a long time in my hometown. Their mentality was simply to ignore the weak, flatter the ones you need to control and kill the ones you can't. This manifested into a Pharisaical mentality in the church. Some of the powerful church leaders did the same, ignoring the weak, flattering the spiritual leaders they wanted to control and killing the reputation of the ones they couldn't control.

However, in the battle, I lost a sense of who I really am called to be. I am not called to wear beige. I am called to be a strong leader. I am not being rebellious or disrespectful when Holy Spirit leads me to speak the truth. I am not being defensive if I state my disagreement with certain ideas. I am under the blood of Christ, not under the curse, so men are not meant to lord over me, regardless of church doctrine. I had to face my fear of man to take my position in Christ. If I allowed my experiences to decide who I was, I would probably be an angry, bitter person by now. Thank you, Jesus, for leading me through the pain of rejection to find peace through forgiveness. Please don't let the pain of life tell you who you are. R.E.A.L. Joy comes in going back to Eden, God's pleasure, to recover your true identity and take your position in Christ.

True Destiny

Once we claim our true identity, then we can begin to activate the gifts of God that are within us. If we know our gifts but not our identity, we will use our gifts selfishly, trying to get the approval of others. The motivational or DNA gifts of Romans 12 are given by the Father so that we can work together as the body of Christ. These gifts are not meant to limit us but rather to help us understand who we are and honor others who have different gifts. Books have been written on the motivational gifts as well as the four personality temperaments. It is absolutely essential to your destiny that you have an experiential knowledge of both. It's not enough to merely know about the DNA gifts and the four temperaments, because intellectual information is easily lost. Study these with those closest to you and use them to develop better communication skills.

The DNA gifts in Romans 12 include; prophet, servant, teacher, exhorter, giver, ruler and mercy. Each gift expresses a unique Kingdom perspective of life, that if properly understood, will help us accomplish our destiny to advance the Kingdom. The devil sows seeds of discord, confusion, jealousy, and bitterness to make sure that we do not produce the fruit of these gifts. When these gifts work together, they make the body of Christ unstoppable! When misunderstood, they can make us reckless and destructive.

Let this encourage you to study this subject at length. If I have the DNA gift of prophet, that does not make me a five-fold prophet (Ephesians 4:11), nor does it alone mean that I will be used by the Holy Spirit to prophesy. Father, Jesus and Holy Spirit all have their own gift lists. Prophet appears in each list, but it means something different, depending on who is giving you the gift.

1. The Father's gift list is in Romans 12, the DNA gifts, where it tells us to use our gift according to our level of faith. This means we possess the gift and have a responsibility to develop it in a mature fashion. If I have the Father's gift of prophet, then I am a very black and white kind of person who is quick to make decisions. It will require me to benefit from the other gifts to mature as a DNA prophet. Many DNA prophets will prophesy, thinking that makes them a five-fold prophet.

2. This is not so. Holy Spirit gives the gift of prophecy in 1 Corinthians 12, along with eight other gifts. But, unlike the Father's gift list, we do not possess these gifts, they are given by Holy Spirit as He wills as situations arise. So I can prophesy by Holy Spirit as a servant, teacher, giver etc., but I am not a prophet simply because I prophesy.

3. Then, what is a five-fold prophet? Jesus gives the five-fold gift of ministry. These gifts include apostle, prophet, pastor, teacher and evangelist. Ephesians 4 explains these are given to equip the saints to do the work of the ministry. A five-fold prophet moves beyond prophesying to equipping others to identify, activate and release prophecy in a spiritually mature and beneficial way. As a five-fold prophet, I will often hold a prophetic word back so that I can make opportunity for those in training to step up to the plate and prophesy. **Not everyone who has the DNA gift of prophet prophesies. Also, not everyone who prophesies is a five-fold prophet. The lack of understanding has caused much confusion instead of joy.** If you want more information on the DNA gifts go to unleashedhealingcenter.com.

Let me give you one more reason to study these gifts. The DNA gift of mercy is not the same as the virtue of mercy. The virtue of mercy is to withhold the judgment someone rightfully deserves. Every believer is called to develop the virtue of mercy but not everyone has the DNA gift from the Father to be a mercy. My son is a mercy which is polar opposite from the DNA prophet. Prophet is first on the list and mercy is last, for good reason. The prophet *thinks* whereas the mercy *feels*. I would ask my son what he was thinking and he would say, "I don't know." It was so frustrating to me as a prophet. How could you not know what you are thinking? But when I learned to ask my son what he was feeling, we started to communicate. Those with the DNA gift of mercy are about being, not doing. Rest is their weapon. They want to move slowly in order to experience the subtleties of life. As a prophet, I look at that and want to tell them to get moving! When I learned to value my son's gift, I started to learn from him as well as become more effective in helping him mature. These gifts aren't labels that limit us, but they are valuable in helping us honor one another and work harmoniously.

Personality Temperaments

Now, what about the four personality temperaments? I have studied the temperaments for years. You've probably taken one of these tests by now. After years of using many different materials out there, I asked Holy Spirit where these temperaments were in scripture. I thought this was too good to not be in the Bible. Holy Spirit directed me to Ezekiel 1. I developed a test based on this passage more than ten years ago. Recently, I heard Lance Wallnau teach on the temperaments from Ezekiel 1, but from a slightly different angle. I was excited to see that Holy Spirit had released this teaching to others. It is an indication of the season that is upon the church, but more on that later.

Ezekiel 1 is the vision of the four creatures that fly around the throne. They each have four faces: the man, the lion, the ox and the eagle. The creatures have two wheels below them that intersect each other and are covered in eyes. Most theologians believe these wheels to represent the sovereignty of God, moving in all directions, seeing everything. Ezekiel states that the Spirit of the Lord was in the creatures — each representing a different temperament — and the spirit of the creatures were in the wheels, so that everywhere the creatures went so went the wheels. God puts His Spirit into our personality temperaments. The different ways our temperaments respond to God affect how His sovereignty moves on the earth. That is some powerful information, and if understood properly, can empower us to change the world.

God put His personality in our temperament, and the way our temperaments respond to God affects how His sovereignity moves on the earth!

Proverbs tells us that we perish because of a lack of knowledge. It is this information about our identity, gifts, and personality that we need so desperately right now. I believe the shift in the church is a call to the Mercy Season: a season in which we are more about being who we truly are than about what we do. It's about rest; slowing down enough to pick up on the subtle but important differences. R.E.A.L. Joy is accelerated when we discover our identity and can give to others, rather than needing something from them. R.E.A.L. Joy is accelerated in our lives when we can honor one another in unity to fulfill destiny.

For more information on the DNA gifts and four personality temperaments you can order, go to unleashedhealingcenter.com or http://getrealliving.com

Chapter 11

Accept You:
Serve Others with Joy

D id you ever see the T.V. show *Gold Rush*? I used to watch it all the time, but then it became hard to watch the character fail over and over again. They had to move so much dirt just to find a small amount of gold. They spent weeks moving worthless dirt before they even got to the pay dirt. Then they would strain the pay dirt with machinery, and the equipment would break down constantly because of the stress placed on them; not to mention their constant stress that affected their communications. Needless to say, it was a lot of work for the payoff.

Well, that is what we are called to do as believers. I call it diamond-hunting. We have to ignore a whole lot of dirt in people's lives to get to the good stuff. It can be rigorous trying to draw out of them what is of value. If we are going to serve others joyfully, we will need to maintain our own identity first or the process will be stressful. Let me share a few principles found in Song of Solomon that will help you serve joyfully and help you understand how to embed them in your ministry culture.

I *am* dark, but lovely, O daughters of Jerusalem, Like the tents of Kedar, Like the curtains of Solomon. Do not look upon me, because I am dark, Because the sun has tanned me. My mother's sons were angry with me; They made me the keeper of the vineyards, *But* my own vineyard I have not kept. (To Her Beloved) Tell me, O you whom I love, Where you feed *your flock,* Where you make *it* rest at noon. For why should I be as one who veils herself By the flocks of your companions? – Song of Solomon 1:5-8 (*NKJV*)

Principle #1: The Dark but Lovely Mandate

"I am dark but lovely."

This passage states clearly the balance between our position in Christ and our experience, as described in the previous chapter. She states, "I am dark" referring to her tan from working the fields — this was a sign of poverty. Yet she also knew that to the king she was "lovely." Every day, we must balance the limitations of our humanity with our position in Christ, which is full of prosperity. If I forget that I am dark, I can become arrogant. If I forget that I am lovely, I can become full of shame and strive in my relationships instead of embracing relationship with God and others.

> *If I forget that I am dark, I become arrogant. If I forget I am lovely, I can become full of shame.*

In the Spirit, I saw this balance similar to remaining in the eye of a tornado. Standing in the eye of the vortex, I noticed an eagle was flying in circles above my head, causing the tornado around me. The Father said, "Stay in line with the eagle and you will stay at rest." As the eagle moved, so did I, but occasionally I would move ahead or lag behind and get swept up into the storm. Father spoke, "The storm is the soulish realm, and the calm, the spirit realm. Holy Spirit has designed this balance to keep you close to Him." I have learned over the years to get better at recognizing when I have leaned too far to one side. The result is the same — either stress and lack of rest or peace and joy in my life and ministry.

Here are a few indicators that you have gotten caught up into the soul realm either by self-reliance or shame:

1. You feel rejected by believers;

2. You feel shame because of sin;

3. You are overworked;

4. You have become distracted from intimacy with Jesus;

5. You are serving Jesus at a distance.

To enter back into rest:

1. Recognize spiritual crisis

2. Identify yourself as a lover of God

3. Seek intimacy with God in the midst of crisis

4. Commit to the body of Christ

5. Submit to your spiritual authority

Principle #2: Tend Your Own Vineyard

"My Mother's sons were angry with me and made me the keeper of the vineyards."

As we continue to look at this passage, we notice another principle for helping us serve others joyfully. In Song of Solomon, "the mother" is the church. Many times when we are helping others or trying to diamond hunt, they can become angry with us because they are not ready or able to receive the truth we know they need. We cannot care more about someone's spiritual life than they do. This is what it means to be an enabler or a control freak. Neither is effective.

Song of Solomon (2:7; 3:5; and 8:4) gives us the solution. Three times Jesus instructs the daughters of Jerusalem, who represent the church as well, to not awaken love before its time. He says, "I charge you." This is not a suggestion. It is a command. He gives the command by the gazelle in 2:7 and 3:5. The gazelle, a very skittish animal, will flee if even slightly startled. In essence, Jesus is trying to guard His children in their immaturity from well-meaning but religious people who operate in fear rather than grace. Jesus is also trying to protect those who are in service. If we try to help people that don't want our help, they will leave offended with us. This doesn't help them and often hurts us as well. We are not the keeper of anyone's vineyard but our own. That leads to the next principle for serving joyfully.

Principle #3: Learn Rest

"But my own vineyard I have not kept. Tell me, o you whom I love, Where you feed *your flock,* where you make *it* rest at noon."

My college professor used to say, "It's easy to get so caught up in the work of our God that we forget the God of our work." We cannot afford to be so busy that we fail to maintain intimacy with Trinity. This involves more than serving Him at a distance. It involves more than a disciplined Bible study time void of true connection with Trinity. We must find the place of rest in God in the middle of our hectic day. He rests His flocks at the noon hour. This is the peak business time. My dad taught me this **acronym for "busy" — Being**

Under Satan's Yoke! We must labor to enter into our rest (Hebrews 11:4). It is a challenge to prioritize rest in a culture that values business above relationship. Jesus says in Matthew 11:28, "Come unto me all you who are weak and heavy with burden and I will give you rest." We have to come to get the rest. He's not coming after us! To accelerate joy in serving others, we must learn to rest.

"For why should I be as one who veils herself by the flocks of your companions?"

In summary, the bride in this passage is realizing that her shame is rooted in self-ambition, self-condemnation and self-preservation. She hides herself because she believes the lies that steal joy: "I must do everything well, everything needs to go well, and everyone needs to treat me well." Finally, she realizes she doesn't have to hide in shame anymore. She learns to stay in balance by accepting that she is dark but lovely. When our service flows out of true identity, it becomes energy-producing, not energy-demanding. **If we are going to find R.E.A.L. Joy, then it must be accelerated by serving others.**

When our service to others flows from true identity in Christ, it becomes energy-producing, not energy-demanding.

Chapter 12

Be You: Accept others, Walk in Unity, Release Joy

I sat with a pastor who was broken and tired. He had great vision but seemed to lose his leadership on a regular basis. He thought he was under attack until he came to me for help. I asked, "What are you doing to show your leaders that you need them and that they are vital to God's vision for the ministry?" He said, "Well, I try to pay the staff well and I do a leader's appreciation banquet. I like to send emails to thank them for what they are doing." I replied, "How do they know you can't do this job without them?" He said, "Well, I am reliant on God, not them." I said, "That's why they can so easily leave without remorse. They know you and God will work it out!" He was puzzled to say the least.

Yes, we are stewards, not owners, of our lives and service to God. He is in control, but He puts us in charge. Men, I know you value independence, so please don't check out on me yet. God is shifting the church into the mercy season, as I mentioned earlier. We are called the body of Christ with Jesus as the head. That means that as a leader and steward of the kingdom, I am a part of the vision and not dictator of it. If I want to develop covenant relationship with leadership, I need to practice "volunteer weakness." We need to choose to depend on others, so we create interdependence, which develops loyalty and commitment.

We need to choose to depend on others so we create interdependence, which develops loyalty and commitment.

So, I asked the pastor who was losing leaders, "What can you turn over to your leaders to do their way instead of yours? What arena can you choose to not lead but let someone on your staff take the lead??" When your leaders come to you with an idea, don't fire-hose it! Don't tell them all the reasons it won't work. Give them room to try and even fail if need be. Then be there to thank them for trying so hard. Also, make it a point to ask your leaders to pray for your personal needs and to even give you advice. Remember, if you know the DNA gifts of those around you, this is easy to do. For instance, I have learned to ask servants to pray for illness. They have an anointing for that. When I get a vision, I rely on the rulers in my leadership to show me the practical steps of that vision. I do not expect to know everything. Instead, I look for opportunity to purposely rely on leaders. Even if I can do it myself, I often don't!

This absolutely flies in the face of conventional wisdom. I was taught in Bible college that familiarity breeds contempt, so to keep a safe distance from the people you serve or they won't respect you. That can happen, but the risk is worth it. My husband and I started our ministry 11 years ago, with eleven adults. Today, every single one of them is still with us. We keep adding leaders every year, and we are up to about 70 leaders. People will come and go, but our leaders, the people in whom we invest our time, talents and treasures… they stay! Over the years, we have only lost one person we trained as a leader, and that was early on. We are better equipped to recognize problems of disunity and deal with them. We have lost five-six people we were expecting to train but didn't. Many people like to talk about the five-fold ministry, but it takes hard work to cultivate it. Developing unity is not for wimps. It takes humility and freedom from the approval and performance traps to cultivate covenant. Membership is easy, but covenant is something else!

Like I said earlier, I learned about developing the five-fold ministry through my family relationships. My father is a five-fold pastor, with the DNA gift of teacher and exhorter. He is amazing with people, especially with developing men. He is a walking Bible concordance. He knows his Word, but his pastor's heart to protect along with his DNA gift of teaching does not motivate him to be a forerunner like me. As a prophet, I hate status quo. A teacher, on the other hand, relies on it. At times, it has been like the clash of the titans between us. He will probably try to talk me out of including some of my crazy stories from this book. You will never know if I listened to him or not! Ha-ha!

My brother is an evangelist who for a long time saw the church service almost solely as a means to reach the lost. He, like many in the body of Christ, thought that intimacy in worship should be in another time and place such as a private prayer meeting in someone's home. Now he sees our vision to keep the church service on Sunday for God and equipping the saints, so we can send the saints equipped to the marketplace to minister the gospel during the week. But it took the kind of covenant relationship we have as sister and brother to work through those differences and develop something that works for all the gifts.

My sister Teri and her husband Paul are second in command at RLM. Teri is a ruler and Paul is a mercy, but they are both fabulous pastors and five-fold teachers in our ministry. As they can receive the vision from Perry and me, they develop a practical plan to implement the vision and the tools to get it into the hearts of our people.

My mother is an amazing servant whose prayer life is largely responsible for everything her family is doing in the ministry. Because of her faithfulness we are seeing the next generation, her grandkids, serve the Lord with passion.

My sister Nicole, cousin Michelle, and friend who's been like a sister, Star, are all in leadership. We are seeing whole families being raised up as leaders such as a mother-daughter team that leads our children's ministry. These amazing blessings have definitely come with challenges, but I wouldn't and probably couldn't do it any other way. It will take R.E.A.L. strength in R.E.A.L. relationships for R.E.A.L. Joy to accelerate through serving others.

Our Miracle Story

Remember when I shared earlier the lessons learned through my daughter Carley's addiction to cutting? Well, it also took the faith and unity of family to see her life spared and gloriously redeemed. I want to end this book by sharing our miraculous story.

One Sunday afternoon on the way home from church Carley and her sister got into a fight. When we pulled in the drive and stopped the car, Carley ran into the house. By the time I got in the door I heard her screaming for help. I ran upstairs to see her covered in blood. She had decided to graduate from scissors to a razor. I was holding her thigh together while screaming for my husband to call 911. There was so much blood I was afraid she would bleed out before they got there! My son Perry, only 10 at the time, stepped into the room and calmly placed his hand on mine. In a loud, authoritative tone he said,

"Satan I command you to take your hands off Carley. I command the bleeding to stop right now!" I was taken aback. It was out of character for him, to say the least, but the bleeding stopped immediately. We were able to take her by car to get stitches.

The calm, loving and safe voice of my husband eased all of our fears on the drive to the hospital. Carley was very repentant for all the hurt she had put us all through. It was evident the spell the enemy had her under was broken at last.

Later, at the hospital, my son shared what he experienced. During worship earlier in the morning, he'd had a vision of a tornado swirling around Carley. The Lord told Him to reach inside the tornado and command it to stop. He did, and the tornado stopped. Therefore, at the right time, he was ready and knew exactly what to do while the rest of us were in panic mode.

When it first happened, Carley had been crying, saying, "Please, Mom, heal me right now." All her anger and doubt were gone; all that remained — faith. Not just faith in God, but trust in me as well. She needed my faith to be added to hers. She needed her mom. I shared with her that she was receiving much more than a physical healing but a spiritual one as well. She never cut again after that day.

In the weeks that followed, my sister Teri, her life coach, gave her the practical tools she needed to heal. It was the intercession of our prophetic team who prayed and covered our family during the whole ordeal.

One such prayer happened a few weeks before the crisis. I had the prophetic team in Carley's room while she was at school. Pastor Judy had a vision of Carley sitting at her vanity, looking in the mirror and saying hateful things to herself. The Lord told Judy to place a veil that was in Carley's closet over the mirror. Carley had been a flower girl years earlier, and it was still in her closet. The others on the team believed the veil would remain there until Carley was ready to be healed. The veil was there as a sign of God's protection over her until she was ready to awaken love.

To be honest, I thought she would take it down as soon as she got home, but she didn't. In fact, she never even asked about it until several days after her hospital experience. I told her why it was there. Several weeks later she removed it. To this day, written in red lipstick on her mirror her favorite scripture reads,

> You are altogether beautiful, my darling; **there is no flaw in you.**
> – Song of Solomon 4:7 (*NIV*)

About a year later, I went with Carley to get her first tattoo; definitely an act of love and support on my part because I'm truly not a fan of tattoos! But her tattoo says in Italian, "Nothing without Family." She had it put on the side of her foot as a reminder of the unity and love it takes to walk out our destiny… joyfully!

Walking in unity is not for wimps, but it brings joy.

A Final Word

I hope you have benefited from this journey to R.E.A.L. Joy. Together we have learned the source of R.E.A.L. Joy is to get R.E.A.L. with God - Responding Entirely to the Affections of the Lord.

It also takes getting R.E.A.L. with self for truth mandates joy and getting R.E.A.L. with others for unity accelerates joy.

I didn't want to be just a travel agent telling you how to get there. I tried to be a tour guide, going with you, through my personal stories. May the joy of the Lord always be your strength.

About the Author

Joy Chickonoski is the Founder and Executive Director of UnLeashed Healing Center, unleashing the heart of the Father, bringing healing for the spirit, soul and body around the world. Along with her husband, Perry Chickonoski, they started Real Living Ministries in 2007, an Apostolic Center, equipping and releasing R.E.A.L. worshippers on mission to the world. Additionally, they serve as national apostolic leaders for the Seven Mountains of Cultural Influence, with Heartland Apostolic Prayer Network (HAPN). Married for 26 plus years, they have three adult children, Carley, Cami and Perry, who each play an active role in their ministry.

Recommended Resources

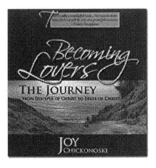

Becoming Lovers – The Journey from Disciple of Christ to Bride of Christ
–Joy Chickonoski (Book) **$10.00**

We are always at the beginning with God, because the journey never ends. We are always a novice no matter how long we have walked with God. This book describes the journey of a true Christian. Each chapter will unfold the stages, struggles and surprises of pursuing Jesus Christ passionately.

Your DNA Design - Test – $30.00

A comprehensive test into the unique DNA gifts the Father has given you

Your DNA Design - Journal – $20.00

Your DNA Design journal - allows you to take a deeper dive into discovering "you"

Your DNA Design - Combo – $45.00

(1) Your DNA Design comprehensive test, and
(2) Your DNA Design journal

To purchase, go to the store at:
unleashedhealingcenter.com

Made in the USA
Columbia, SC
01 September 2024

40882030R00109